FORWARD

This manual has been written for the purpose of helping ministers and church officials better understand the income tax rules as they apply to ministers and churches. After becoming familiar with the information contained in this manual, the individual will find him or her self more knowledgeable in reference to the income tax rules that govern ministers and churches.

This manual has been written with the understanding that it is not a legal document nor is it intended to completely replace the services one would receive from an Accountant, Attorney, or Tax Professional. Therefore, after familiarizing yourself with the information contained in this manual, if you require additional assistance, please seek this assistance from an Accountant, Attorney, or Tax Professional.

Alston Business Concepts & Development Systems, Inc., Publisher
K. L. Alston, Author

Columbia, South Carolina

Things You Should Know Before & After Becoming a Minister

For information address K. L. Alston, K.L. Alston Enterprises, P.O. Box 50581, Columbia, South Carolina 29250.

Table of Contents

INTRODUCTION

It is the responsibility of both the minister and the church (Minister, Church Officials, etc.) to insure that the revenue (Income) and expenditures (expenses) of the church as well as the wages for employees are correctly accounted for and correctly reported. Establishing a proper accounting system and selecting the correct forms and documents are a very important part of this responsibility as well as understanding the two systems (FICA and SECA) Social Security and Medicare taxes are collected under. Under the Federal Insurance Contributions Act (FICA), the employee pays part of the tax, and the employer pays part of the tax. Under the Self-Employment Contributions Act (SECA), the self-employed individual is required to pay the entire tax amount due. No earnings are subject to taxation under both systems.

In this manual, I will define and explain the status of a minister, earnings for ministers, which earnings are taxed under FICA, and which earnings are taxed under SECA. I will also discuss the federal laws and guidelines for churches and ministers, housing and parsonage allowances, church reporting requirements, legal forms and documents, preferred tax forms and the purpose of these forms as recommended by the Internal Revenue Service, how to calculate net earnings from self-employment, how ministers can apply for an exemption from self-employment tax, and a host of other pertinent information ministers and church officials need to know to assist them with staying within IRS and reporting compliance.

WHO QUALIFIES AS A MINISTER

A minister by definition is an individual who is duly ordained, commissioned, or licensed to the pastoral ministry by action of a religious body constituting a church or church denomination. This individual has been given the authority to conduct religious worships, to perform sacerdotal functions and to administer ordinances or sacraments according to the prescribed tenets and principles of that church or church denomination.

In order for an individual, for federal tax purposes, to be considered a minister, there are five factors that must be considered:

1. The individual must be ordained, commissioned, or licensed,
2. They must conduct religious worship,
3. They must have management responsibilities in the local church or a parent denomination,
4. They must be considered a religious leader by the church or parent
   Denomination,
5. They must perform sacerdotal functions and administer

ordinances or sacraments according to the prescribed tenets and principles of that church or church denomination.

The Internal Revenue Service and the tax courts require that a minister be licensed, ordained, or commissioned. After that, the other four factors will be weighed in. The more of the other four factors the individual satisfies, the more likely that individual will be deemed a minister for tax reporting purposes.

EMPLOYMENT STATUS

The question of whether a minister is an employee of the church or self-employed has created some confusion for quite sometime. The fact of the matter is most ministers have what is considered a "dual tax status." For federal income tax purposes, ministers are employees. However, for social security purposes (with respect to the services ministers perform in the exercise of their ministry), ministers are **always** considered self-employed. As an employee, the church should report the earnings paid to a minister on the Form W-2. Due to the fact that a minister is always considered self-employed for social security purposes, the federal income tax, social security tax, Medicare tax, and state income tax withheld boxes should remain blank.

The distinction between a minister being classified as an employee or a self-employed individual is determined on the grounds of the "common law" rules. In making this distinction, "employer control over the manner in which the work is performed either actual or the right to it, is the basic test." In other words, the employer need not exercise control over the manner in which the work is performed, the mere fact that the employer has the right to control the employee when it is appropriate and deemed necessary is all that is required to meet the qualification of control. It is extremely important that the absence of the need to control the manner in which the minister performs his or her ministerial duties is not confused with the absence of the **right** to control.

EMPLOYMENT STATUS OF A MINISTER

As the minister of a church, the earnings the minister receives for the services performed in the capacity as a minister are subject to self-employment tax. This is the case unless the minister has submitted a Form 4361 (Application for Exemption From Self-Employment Tax for Use by Ministers, Members of Religious Orders, and Christian Science Practitioners) to the Internal Revenue Service, and been approved for the exemption by the Internal Revenue Service. Form 4361 will be discussed in more detail later. The income the minister receives in his or her capacity as a minister will **always** be subject to self-employment tax for social security tax purposes whether the minister is an employee for federal income tax purposes, or a self-employed person under the common law rules.

Even though a minister is **always** considered self-employed for social security tax purposes, under common law rules a minister may or may not be considered self-employed for federal income tax purposes. Under common law rules, a minister will be considered an employee or self-employed based upon certain conditions and/or circumstances. Generally, a minister will be considered an employee if his or her employer has the legal right to control both what he or she does, and the manner in which he or she does it. This is the case even if the minister has considerable discretion and freedom of action in performing these duties. If a congregation for a salary employs a minister, generally the minister will be considered a common-law employee, and the income from the exercise of him or her performing his or her duties as a minister will be considered income for federal income tax purposes. This is the case only for the income the minister receives in performing the duties as a minister for his or her church. If a minister receives income directly from congregants such as fees for performing marriages, baptisms, or other personal services, that income received may be considered self-employment income, and is not related to the income the minister receives from his or her church.

***Example* 1.** *Reverend Alston is hired by a church, and is paid a* *salary to perform ministerial services subject to the church's control. Based upon common-law rules, Reverend Alston is an employee of the church while performing his Ministerial services.*

***Example* 2.** *A couple who are members of the church that has hired Reverend Alston, and pays him a salary to perform ministerial services subject to the church's control hires Reverend Alston to perform their marriage ceremony. They pay Reverend Alston $50.00. The $50.00 received by Reverend Alston is considered self-employment income.*

STATUTORY AND NONSTATUTORY RULES

Due to statutory law, a minister is considered to be a self-employed individual in performing ministerial services for social security tax purposes. However, because of common law or non-statutory law rules, a minister can be considered an employee for federal income taxes or retirement tax purposes.

Under Common Law or Non-statutory Rules, an individual is considered an employee or a self-employed individual based on the circumstances. Generally, an individual is an employee if his of her employer has the legal right to control both what he or she does and how he or she does it, even if the individual has considerable discretion and freedom of action.

DETERMINING THE EMPLOYMENT STATUS OF A MINISTER

In actuality, determining the status of a minister is only done for federal income tax purposes. Remember, for social security tax purposes, a minister is **always** considered self-employed. However, that does not make it any less important. The status of the minister will dictate how related expenses will be accounted for and deducted on the minister's income tax return. If a minister is deemed an employee for federal income tax purposes, then all un-reimbursed expenses will have to be deducted on the Form 2106, and then transferred to the Form Schedule A where they are subject to a two percent floor. This means the minister will have to be able to itemize his or her deductions. In order to utilize the Form Schedule A, an individual's itemized deductions must exceed his or her standard deduction. Second, in order to receive any benefits from the deduction, only the amount that is greater than two percent of the individual's adjusted gross income will be deductible. On the other hand, if the income a minister receives is deemed self-employment income, all related expenses are deductible on the Form Schedule C. In this manner, the minister will receive the entire benefit of the deductions because there isn't a two percent floor to take into consideration. The differences in the two would produce a noticeable difference in the minister's income taxes liability.

***Example* 1.** *For federal income tax purposes, Reverend Alston is deemed an employee. During the tax year, Reverend Alston accumulates $1,500 worth of un-reimbursed employee expenses. Reverend Alston's adjusted gross income is $60,000. Of the $1,500 worth of un-reimbursed employee expenses, only $300 of his un-reimbursed employee expenses will be deductible. $60,000 times 2% = $1,200 (2% Floor equals $1,200); $1,500 minus- $1,200 = $300 ($300 Deductible Expenses)*

***Example* 2.** *For federal income tax purposes, the income Reverend Alston received is deemed self-employment income. During the tax year, in association with earning the above income, Reverend Alston accumulated $1,500 worth of expenses. The entire $1,500 is deductible on the Form Schedule C (Net Profit From Business) as business expenses, and is not subject to a 2% floor.*

To assist in making the distinction, there are four different tests that can be utilized when determining the employment status of a minister. This is extremely important not only because of federal income tax reasons but also for Internal Revenue Service reclassification reasons. If a minister files as a self-employed individual and is audited by the Internal Revenue Service, if it is found during the audit that the minister was actually an employee for federal income tax purposes, the Internal Revenue Service can reclassify the minister as an employee. If the Internal Revenue Service ever reclassifies a minister from the status of self-employed to the status of an employee, the results could prove very costly to the minister. For example, if a minister is reclassified the expenses the minister had initially deducted on his or her income tax return as business expenses on the Form Schedule C would no longer be deductible as business expenses. Therefore, instead of receiving a 100% deduction, the expenses would become deductible as un-reimbursed employee expenses, and un-reimbursed employee expenses are deductible as itemized deductions, and are subject to a 2% floor as explained above.

***Example* 1.** *Reverend Alston filed his previous year's income tax return as a self-employed individual. His earnings from the church totaled $30,000. His business expenses totaled $10,000. Therefore, Reverend Alston showed a net profit of $20,000. Reverend Alston's self-employment tax was calculated based upon his net profit of $20,000. Reverend Alston is audited by the Internal Revenue Service and reclassified as an employee. The deductions Reverend Alston deducted as business expenses are no longer deductible as business expenses. The $10,000 now becomes un-reimbursed employee expenses, which are deductible as itemized deductions, and are subject to a 2% floor. Reverend Alston's self-employment tax is now calculated based upon his earnings of $30, 000.*

If a minister or lay worker is in doubt in regards to his or her employee status, Form SS-8 (Determination of Employee Work Status for Purposes of Federal Employment Taxes and Income tax Withholding) can be submitted to the Internal Revenue Service to get a determination. There are at least four (4) tests that are utilized to determine the status of an individual. They include: The "common law employee" test; The "20 factor" test; The "7 factor" test; and The "12 factor" test.

The "common law employee" test is one of the most frequently used tests by the Internal Revenue Service and the tax courts. This test basically deals with the issue of the right-to-control in reference to the employer-employee relationship.

The IRS "20 factor" test was developed "as an aid in determining whether an individual is an employee under the common law rules." *Revenue Ruling* 87- 41. The 20 factors are as follows:

1. Instructions - An individual who has to comply with instructions about when, where, and how to work is ordinarily an employee.
2. Training - Training of an individual by an experienced employee or by other means is a factor of control and indicates an employee status.

3. Integration - Integration of an individual's services into the business operations generally displays that the individual is subject to direction and control and is therefore an employee.
4. Services Rendered Personally - If the services must be provided by the individual personally, it may suggests an employer-employee relationship. Normally when an individual is self-employed, he or she has the right to hire a substitute without the employer's knowledge.
5. Hiring, supervising, and paying assistants - Hiring, supervising, and payment of assistants by an employer normally indicates that the workers on the job are employees.
6. Continuing relationship - If after the individual has performed the required services the existence of a continuing relationship between the individual and the company or organization develops, this may indicate an employer-employee relationship.
7. Set hours of work - The establishment of set hours to work by the employer is an indication of an employer-employee relationship.
8. Full time required - If the employer establishes the worker must devote full time to the business, the worker is ordinarily an employee.
9. Performing the work on the employer's premises - Performing the job on the employer's premises may indicate an employee status especially if the work can be performed somewhere else.

10. Order or sequence of work - If the employer controls the sequence or order of the work being performed, this indicates employee status.
11. Oral or written report - If the employer requires the worker to submit written or oral reports regularly, an employer-employee relationship may exist.
12. Payment by hour, week, or month - Employees are normally paid by the hour, week, or month.
13. Payment of business expenses - If the employer pays the worker's business or travel expenses, an employer-employee relationship may exist.
14. Furnishing of tools and materials - When an employer furnishes the tools and materials, this indicates an employer-employee relationship.
15. Significant investment - The employer furnishing all the necessary equipment and premises displays an employer-employee relationship.
16. Realization of profit or loss - Not being in a position to realize a profit or a loss indicates an employee status.
17. Working for more than one firm at a time - A self-employed individual usually works for more that one firm at a time.
18. Making services available to the general public - Normally, individuals who offer their services to the general public are self-employed.
19. Right to discharge - An employer normally cannot fire a self-

employed individual as long as the work is being performed based upon the contractual agreement.

20. Right to terminate - Ordinarily an employee can terminate the relationship with an employer at any time without incurring liability.

The Tax Court's "7 factor" test factors are as follows:

1. The degree of employer control over the worker,
2. Which party invests in the facilities utilized to perform the work,
3. The opportunity for profit or loss for the worker,
4. Whether the employer has the right to discharge the worker,
5. Whether the work being performed is a part of the employer's regular business,
6. The permanency of the relationship that exists between the employer and the worker,
7. The relationship the employer and worker believe they are creating.

The Supreme Court's "12 factor" test factors are as follows:

1. The employer's rights in regards to controlling the manner in which the job will be performed and completed,
2. The source providing the tools and supplies that will be

utilized to complete the work,

3. The location from which the work will be performed,
4. The duration of the relationship between the employer and the worker,
5. The employer's right to assign additional projects to the worker,
6. The employer's control in regards to the amount of time it will take the worker to complete the job,
7. The payment method,
8. The employer's role in regards to hiring the worker,
9. The employer's role in regards to paying the worker,
10. Whether the work being performed is a part of the regular business of the employer,
11. Whether the employer in business,
12. The benefits the worker receives.

RECLASSIFICATION

Ministers who report their federal income taxes as self-employed face a greater risk of additional taxes and penalties if they are ever audited, by the Internal Revenue Service, and reclassified as an employee. Reason being, ministers who file their taxes as self-employed utilize a Schedule C to deduct their expenses and receive the full benefit of the deduction. If reclassification occurs, those expenses will only be allowed as itemized deductions on the Form Schedule A. **In** addition, only the amount of the expenses that exceed

2% of the adjusted gross income will be deductible. For those ministers who cannot itemize, they will lose the deduction completely. **In** addition, the consequences of treating an employee of the church as an independent contractor could prove costly to the church if an individual is reclassified from independent contractor status to employee status.

SPECIAL TAX PROVISIONS FOR MINISTERS

Individuals who qualify as ministers for federal tax purposes are eligible for four special tax rules with respect to the services they perform in the exercise of their ministry.

1. Housing or parsonage allowance exclusion,
2. Exemption from self-employment taxes providing several conditions are met,
3. Self-employed status for social security purposes,
4. Wages are exempt from federal income tax withholdings.

ALLOWANCE (Parsonage, Rental and Housing)

Typically, a minister is involved in one of three housing arrangements. A minister can either live in a parsonage provided by the church, receive a "rental allowance" which is used to rent a home, or receive a "housing allowance" which is used to purchase a home. Section 107 of the Internal Revenue Code authorizes the exclusion from ordinary compensation (income reported on the form W - 2) and federal income taxes the fair rental value of a church-provided parsonage which the church may provide to a minister rent-free, or the portion of a minister's compensation that has been designated as a parsonage, rental, or housing allowance. It is very important that the designation of a parsonage, rental, or housing allowance be done in writing, in advance of or as close to the beginning of the calendar year as possible, and adopted by the body of the church that approves compensation (Church Board, Church Congregation, etc.). When designating a parsonage, rental, or housing allowance, the Internal Revenue Service tax regulations specify that the designation may be contained in "an employment contract, in minutes of or in a resolution by a church or other qualified organization or in its budget, or in any other appropriate instrument evidencing such official action." The church employing the minister should make the designation in advance of the first payment. If the minister's employment is by the local church, the local church must make the designation. The national body of that church cannot make the designation. The national body of that local church can only make effective designations for ministers it employs directly.

As stated above, the designation should be made in advance of or as close to the beginning of the calendar year as possible. If the designation is not done prior to the beginning of the calendar year, although there is no penalty imposed on the church nor the minister, there could be a substantial affect in reference to the tax benefit the minister would have received. The longer it takes for the designation to be made, the greater the affect. Simply stated, the total amount of the allowance the minister received prior to the designation being made will have to be reported as compensation. Even though those payment may have been for some type of housing allowance. This will undoubtedly increase the minister's income tax liability at income tax filing time. However, once the designation has been made, the tax benefit becomes effective from that date until the end of the calendar year. The minister cannot include any amount that is retroactive. Any retroactive amounts will be considered compensation for W -2 and federal income tax reporting.

***Example* 1.** *The designation of $1,000 per month is made, in writing, in March of the calendar year for the minister's housing allowance. Since the $1,000 designation was not made in writing until March, the minister has to include as ordinary compensation the $2,000 he or she received in January and February of that calendar year. Since there is no prove of a designation having been made, the amounts received prior to the written designation in March must be included as compensation on the minister's W - 2.*

Amending the original allowance during the year is permissible if the original amount designated proves to be insufficient. However, the new amount is not retroactive. The new amount designated is effective from the date of its designation.

***Example* 2.** *The church designates $800.00 per month as a housing allowance for its minister starting in January of the calendar year. After four months, it becomes apparent that the $800.00 per month will not be enough for the entire year. The housing allowance is amended to $1,000.00 per month. The $1,000.00 is not retroactive to January. The $1,000.00 becomes effective in April. January thru March should still be recorded as $800.00 per month.*

The exclusion of the parsonage, rental, or housing allowance from ordinary compensation and federal income taxes may not appear to be a tax benefit for ministers because it is not a direct credit against the tax liability. But, it is a tremendous benefit because hundreds or even thousand of dollars in taxes can be saved depending upon the amount of the allowance. By not having to include the amount in the first place as compensation, federal income taxes are never calculated. However, although the parsonage, rental, or housing allowance is not utilized when calculating the minister's federal income tax liability, the amount of the allowance has to be included when calculating the minister's self-employment tax.

ALLOWANCES (Housing Expenses) & The Clergy Housing Clarification Act of 2002

Prior to the passing of the "Clergy Housing Clarification Act of 2002", section 107 of the Internal Revenue Code provided that a minister of the gospel could exclude from his or her gross income: (1) the rental value of a home furnished as part of his or her compensation; or (2) the rental allowance paid as part of his or her compensation, to the extent used to rent or provide a home. Section 107 of the income tax code allowed a minister to exclude a housing allowance to the extent that it was utilized to rent or provide a home. Because of Section 107, there was no requirement that the expenses be business related. The only requirement was that the expenses be incurred to rent or provide a home. Although the majority of housing expenses would be incurred for personal reasons and appear to have nothing to do with the minister's profession, they were still excludable as a part of the minister's housing allowance because they were housing related. Housing expenses such as mortgage payments, taxes, insurance, electricity, the base telephone charge, natural gas, and water were fully excludable from ordinary compensation providing these expenses did not exceed the designated housing allowance. The Internal Revenue Service's position (Rev Ruling 71 - 280, 1971 - 2 C.B.92) is that the amount of the section 107 rental allowance that could be excluded from a minister of the gospel's income may not exceed the fair rental value of the home plus the cost of utilities. The case of *Warren* v. *Commissioner,* 114 T.C. No. 23 (2000) prompted new legislation to address any misconceptions and abuse of the Internal Revenue Service's section 107. In this case, according to court documents, the Reverend Richard Warren of the Saddleback Valley Community Church in Orange County, California utilized section 107 of the Internal Revenue Service code to shelter almost all of his compensation from the church from income taxes. In fact, during the years in question, the majority of Reverend Warren's annual compensation from the church was designated as a housing allowance. During a three-year period, of the $87,830 a year Reverend Warren averaged in salary, an average of $77,990 was treated as a tax-exempt housing allowance leaving an average of $9,840 to be reported as taxable salary each year. Due to the fact that he had substantial outside income, more than $200,000 a year on average from the sale of religious books he wrote and tapes he made during the three-year period, he could afford to spend the majority of his church compensation on housing. In fact, Reverend Warren used the housing allowance for mortgage payments and property taxes on his $360,000 home. In addition, he utilized the housing allowance for homeowner’s insurance, utilities, furniture, landscaping, and repairs and maintenance. However, Internal Revenue Service attempted to limit Reverend Warren's tax-exemption to what was equivalent to the fair market value of the house plus the cost of utilities. This was significantly less than what Reverend Warren had spent so the case went to court. The Tax Court ruled in favor of Reverend Warren, and stated that the Internal Revenue Service code section 107- rental allowance exclusion is limited to the amount used to provide the home, and not the fair rental value of the home. The Internal Revenue Service appealed to the United States Court of Appeals for the ninth circuit where the justices took a more fundamental approach in reference to finding a resolution. The justices posed the question of whether the parsonage tax-exemption allowance violated the First Amendment doctrine relating to the separation of church and state. This approach put the entire clergy tax exemption in jeopardy, and the possibility of losing the exemption completely became an Issue. The lost of such a benefit for ministers of the gospel would create a substantial increase in the minister's income tax liability during income tax filing time. Fully understanding the loss of such a benefit for ministers, church groups lobbied Congress to take action, and lawmakers drafted a legislation adopting the Internal Revenue Service's position that the parsonage allowance exemption cannot exceed "the fair rental value of the home, including furnishings and appurtenances such as garage, plus the cost of utilities." This was done so that the Internal Revenue Service would drop its appeal thus preventing the tax-exemption from becoming a constitutional issue. The legislation is called the Clergy Housing Clarification Act of 2002 (H.R. 4156) and is generally applicable for taxable years beginning after December 31, 2001. The provision also applies to taxable years beginning before

January 1, 2002, for which the taxpayer: (1) filed a tax return before April 17, 2002, indicating that the section 107 rental allowance exclusion is limited to the fair rental value of the home (including furnishings and appurtenances) plus the cost of utilities; or (2) files a return after April 16, 2002. Other tax returns for taxable years beginning before January 1, 2002, are not subject to the fair rental value limitation added by the bill.

EXEMPTION FROM SELF-EMPLOYMENT TAX

A minister who has not taken a vow of poverty can request an exemption from self-employment tax. If the request for exemption is approved, it only applies to earnings the minister receives for qualified services. Qualified services are services performed in the exercise of the minister's ministry or, in the exercise of the duties as required by the minister's religious order. The exemption does not apply to any other self-employment income.

***Example* 1.** *Reverend Alston is approved for exemption from self-employment tax. Reverend Alston has a business. Reverend Alston's income from his church is $36,000. Reverend Alston's income from his business is $70,000. The income Reverend Alston received from his church is exempt from self-employment tax, however the income Reverend Alston received from his business is not.*

In order to claim the exemption from self-employment tax, a minister must meet all of the following conditions:

1. File Form 4361,
2. Be conscientiously opposed to public insurance because of your individual religious considerations (not because of your general conscience), or be opposed because of the principles of your religious denomination,
3. File for other than economic reasons,
4. Inform the ordaining, commissioning, or licensing body of your church or order that you are opposed to public insurance if you are a minister or a member of a religious order (other than a vow-of-poverty-member),
5. Establish that the organization that ordained, commissioned, or licensed you or your religious order is a tax-exempt religious organization,
6. Establish that the organization is a church or a convention or association of churches, and
7. Sign and return the statement the Internal Revenue Service mails to you verifying that you are requesting an exemption based on the grounds listed on the statement.

FORM 4361

If a minister did not previously elect to be covered under social security and wishes to be exempt from self-employment tax, Form 4361 (Application for Exemption of Religious Orders and Christian Science Practitioners) must be filed with the Internal Revenue Service. This form includes a statement certifying that the minister opposes, for his or her services as a member of the clergy, public (Governmental) insurance for death, disability, old age, or retirement because of his or her conscience or religious principles. This also includes insurance that helps pay for or provide services for medical care and includes benefits from a system established by the Social Security Act.

The Form 4361 is to be filed by the due date (plus extension) of the tax return for the second year with at least $400.00 of net earnings from self-employment (at least part from qualified services). Once filed, approved, and an approval copy is received from the Internal Revenue Service, it is effective for all tax years after 1967 with at least $400.00 of net warnings from self-employment. The two years do not have to be consecutive and it is important to file Form as soon as possible because it can take some time to receive approval.

MEMBERS OF RECOGNIZED RELIGIOUS SECTS AND FORM 4029

If an individual is a member of a recognized religious sect or a division of a recognized religious sect, an exemption from self-employment tax on all the individual's self-employment income can be obtained by filing Form 4029 (Application for Exemption From Social Security and Medicare Taxes and Waiver of Benefits). If the individual has received social security benefits or payments or anyone else has received these benefits or payments based on the individual's wages of self-employment income, the individual cannot apply for this exemption.

However, if the benefits received are paid back, this individual may be considered for exemption. To find out the amount to be paid back, the local Social Security office can be contacted. To claim the exemption from self-employment tax, all of the following conditions must be met for eligibility:

1. File Form 4029
2. As a follower of the established teachings of the sect or division, you must be conscientiously opposed to accepting benefits of any private or public insurance that makes payments for death, disability, old age, retirement, or

medical care, or provides services for medical care.

3. You must waive all rights to receive any social security payment of benefits and agree that no benefits or payments will be made based on your wages and self-employment income to anyone else.
4. The Secretary of Health and Human Services must determine that:
    1. Your sect or division has such established teachings,
    2. It is the practice and has been for a substantial period of time for members of the sect or division to provide for their dependent members in a manner that is reasonable in view of the members' general level of living, and
    3. The sect or division has existed at all times since December 31, 1950.

If previous approval for exemption from self-employment tax has been received, the individual is considered to have met the requirements and does not need to apply for this exemption.

FORM 4029

Form 4029 can be filed at any time and an approved exemption generally is effective for all tax years beginning after 1950. The exemption does not apply to any tax year beginning before you meet the eligibility requirements. If the individual fails to meet the requirements or the Secretary determined that the sect or division fails to meet the requirements, the exemption will end. If any occurrences that result in the individual no longer being a member of the religious group or if the individual is no longer following the established teachings of the group, the individual must notify the Internal Revenue Service within 60 days. The exemption will end effectively with the date the individual notifies the Internal Revenue Service.

INCOME TAX WITHHOLDING

A minister is not exempt from paying federal income taxes. A minister is exempt from federal income tax withholdings. This is the case regardless of if the minister reports his or her income as an employee or as a self-employed individual. If the minister elects to report his or her income as an employee, the minister may request to have "voluntary withholding" of his or her federal income taxes and self-employment taxes. Under the voluntary withholding arrangement, the minister gives his or her consent for the church to withhold federal income taxes from his or her wages. The church is only obligated to withhold the minister's federal income tax liability.

***Example* 1.** *Reverend Alston is paid a salary of $45,000 from his church. The church is not responsible for withholding any payroll taxes. The federal, social security, Medicare, and state income tax withheld boxes should remain blank. Only the wages paid to Reverend Alston will be reported on his Form W-2.*

***Example* 2.** *Reverend Alston is paid a salary of $45,000 from his church. He has requested to have a voluntary withholding of $300 per pay period withheld from his pay. The church should report the total amount of the voluntary withholding, on Reverend Alston's Form W-2. The amount should appear in the Federal Income Tax Withheld box.*

If a minister has not elected to have voluntary withholding of the federal and self-employment taxes, the minister must pay the federal and self-employment taxes in the form of estimated tax payments. These estimated tax payments must be paid in quarterly installments ***(lst Quarter = Jan, Feb, Mar: Due Date= Apr. 30; 2nd Quarter = Apr, May, Jun: Due Date July* 31; *3rd Quarter = Jul, Aug, Sep: Due Date Oct.* 31; *4th Quarter = Oct, Nov, Dec: Due Date Jan.* 31)** utilizing the Form 1040ES. Remember, although a minister may be deemed an employee for federal tax reasons, a minister is always considered self-employed for social security tax purposes.

EARNINGS FOR MINISTERS

Generally, for the purpose of income taxes a minister is treated as an employee of his or her church. The income a minister receives for performing ministerial services as well as the offerings and fees a minister may receive for performing baptismals, marriages or funerals are all treated as taxable wages as long these services are performed as a requirement of his or her church. However, if services such as baptismals, marriages, or funerals are performed and the minister receives the fee directly from members of the congregation the income received by the minister is considered to be self-employment income. Offerings such as "Love Offerings" given to the church for the benefit of the minister are considered part of the minister's salary if they are exchanged for the minister's services. If these offerings are given to the minister and are not connected to performance or services, the offerings may be considered a gift to the minister and gifts given to an individual are not taxable nor are they deductible as a charitable contribution by the giver.

Example 1. *A love offering of $200 is given to the church on behalf of the minister. The offering is considered part of the minister's income therefore the person given the offering may deduct the $200* *as a charitable contribution providing he or she can utilize the Form Schedule A.*

Example 2. *An individual gives a minister a love offering of $200. The $200 offering is in no way connected to the minister's performance of service. The $200 offering may be considered a gift therefore it is not treated as taxable income to the minister. However, due to the nature of it being a gift, the individual who gave the $200 can not deduct it as a charitable contribution even if he or she can utilize the Form Schedule A.*

For social security tax purposes, a minister is always considered self-employed. Therefore, unless the minister has elected out of Social Security only for his or her ministerial income, the minister is subject to self-employment tax. As for the church, the church is not required to withhold federal income taxes nor social security of Medicare taxes on the minister according to Internal Revenue Service Code 1402 (a) (8). However, a minister does have the option of giving the church authorization to withhold from each pay period an estimated amount of taxes sufficient for both the self-employment and income tax liability. If the minister selects this option, it will alleviate estimated tax payments that are required by the Internal Revenue Service and paid in quarterly installments from all self-employed individuals.

In general, the most significant source of income for a minister is the compensation he or she receives for performing the ministerial duties as prescribed by the church that has hired the minister. For ministers who are employees for federal income tax purposes, this income is received in the form of wages and is reported on line 7 on the Form 1040. For ministers who are self-employed for federal income tax purposes, this income is considered to be self-employment earnings and is reported on the Form Schedule C. Income earned by a minister does not always come in the form of wages. Ministerial compensation can often consists of other items besides salary and some of these other types of compensation must also be included on the minister's W-2 for income tax purposes.

OTHER FORMS OF COMPENSATION

Bonuses, special gifts, fees paid directly to the minister for performing weddings, funerals, baptisms, and masses, monies for travel and other business related expenses that have been allocated under a non-accountable plan and any amounts paid directly by the church in addition to salary to cover the minister's self-employment or income tax all constitute a form of compensation. In order to gain a better perspective into the different types of compensation listed above, we will address each one individually.

Bonuses - Any bonus paid to a minister or member of the church's staff for outstanding work or some other type of achievement is income and must be included as taxable income on the Form W -2 if the individual is reporting his or her federal income taxes as an employee or on the Form 1099 if the individual is reporting his or her taxes as self-employed.

Special Gifts - In some cases, ministers receive special gifts during the course of the year. Some examples are Christmas, birthday, and anniversary gifts. Are these types of gifts considered income that should be reported on the minister's Form W2? Should any type of gift a minister receives be reported as additional income on the minister's Form W-2? Section 102 of the Internal Revenue Code states that "gross income does not include the value of property acquired by gift." This question is not an easy question to answer not even for the Tax Courts. However, the United States Supreme Court did attempt to shed some light onto this matter by noting that "a gift in the statutory sense ... proceeds from a detached and disinterested generosity ... out of affection, respect, admiration, charity, or like impulses. The most critical consideration ... is the transferor's intention. *Commissioner* v. *Dub erste in,* 363 *U.S.* 278, 285 *(1960).*

In another ruling the Supreme Court provided further assistance in distinguishing between a tax-free gift and taxable compensation. It stated, "What controls is the intention with which payment, however voluntary, has been made. Has it been made with the intention that services rendered in the past shall be requited more completely, though full a quittance has been given? If so, it bears a tax. Has it been made to show good will, esteem, or kindliness toward persons who happen to have served, but who are paid without thought to make requital for the service? If so, it is exempt." *Bogardus* v. *Commissioner, 302 U.S.* 34, 45 (1936).

Members are at liberty to make personal gifts to ministers whenever they wish, however such a payment may constitute a tax-free gift and since a tax-free gift is not reported as income by the minister, the member presenting the personal gift can not use the amount as a charitable deduction on his or her income taxes. However, special gift contributions to a minister that have been funded through members' contributions to the church by having been entered or recorded in the church's accounting books as cash received and the contributing members having all received charitable contribution credit, should be reported as taxable compensation on the minister's Form W-2 or Form 1099, and is deductible by the member as a charitable contribution on the Form Schedule A.

Weddings. Funerals. Baptisms. and Masses - The income a minister receives for performing ministerial services as well as the offerings and fees a minister may receive for performing a baptismal, marriages or funerals are all treated as taxable wages as long these services are performed as a requirement of his or her church. However, if these services are performed and the minister receives the fee directly from members of the congregation, the income received by the minister is considered to be self-employment income and should be reported independently of the minister's compensation received for his or her church.

Travel and Other Business Related Expenses That Have Been Allocated Under a Reimbursement Plan - It is very important that the minister as well as church officials understand the differences between a non-accountable reimbursement plan and an accountable-reimbursement plan. A reimbursement plan is a system by which you substantiate and pay the advances, reimbursements, and charges for your employees' business expenses. How reimbursements or allowances are reported depend on whether the plan is an accountable or a non-accountable plan.

Accountable plan: To be an accountable-plan, the reimbursement or allowance arrangement must require the employee to meet all three of the following rules.

1) They must have paid or incurred deductible expenses while performing services as your employees.
2) They must adequately account to you for these expenses within a reasonable period of time.
3) They must return any amounts in excess of expenses within a reasonable period of time.

Amounts paid under an accountable-plan are not wages and are not subject to income tax withholding and payment of social security, Medicare, and federal unemployment taxes.

Non-accountable plan: Payments to employees for travel and other necessary expenses of the business under a non-accountable plan are wages and subject to income tax withholding and payment of social security, Medicare, and FUTA taxes. Your payments are treated as paid under a non-accountable plan if:

1) Your employee is not required to or does not substantiate timely those expenses to you with receipts or other documentation, or
2) You advance an amount to your employee for business expenses and your employee is not required to or does not return timely any amount he or she does not use for business expenses.

Debt Forgiveness Creates Taxable Income - A pastor borrows money from the church to help with the down payment to purchase a new home. Several years later, the pastor accepts a position elsewhere and leaves the church. The loan is never repaid and eventually the board of the church votes to forgive the debt (principle and interest). The amount of debt forgiven constitutes taxable income and should be reported by the pastor. Both the Internal Revenue Service and Tax Court agree that when a debt is forgiven or discharged, the newly freed asset constitutes income since it has become available for the taxpayer's use and enjoyment. The exception to this rationale is filing bankruptcy. If a taxpayer files bankruptcy, the discharge of the debt does not constitute income. *Johnson* v. *Commissioner, 77 RCM 2005* (1999)

Amounts Paid Directly By The Church To Cover The Minister's Self-Employment Tax - Ministers pay a much higher social security tax than regular employees. Because of this, a church may agree to pay an additional amount to cover their minister's self-employment tax liability. This is perfectly legal, however any amount paid to the minister to assist with the minister's self-employment tax must be reported as additional compensation and reported on the minister's Form W-2 or Form 1099 and the minister's Form 1040. The additional amount paid must also be included as compensation for social security purposes as well.

In some cases, the church may give the minister property without charge. The property may be in the form of an automobile, equipment, or a home. The acceptance of such property constitutes income for the minister and must be reported on the minister's Form W-2 or Form 1099. The value of the property and the amount to report as compensation is derived by determining the fair market value of the property and subtracting from that amount any amount paid by the minister for the property. **In** other situations, a church may provide a loan to its ministers however the interest rate of the loan may be extremely low or there may not be an interest rate at all. When a church provides a low-interest or no-interest loan to a minister, not only may the results be additional compensation to the minister, the church providing the loan may be in violation of state nonprofit corporation law. **In** some states, nonprofit corporation laws prohibit churches that are incorporated from providing loans to its ministers and/or directors even if the interest rate of the loan is within the current market standards. **In** addition, low interest or no-interest loans to ministers or directors could be viewed as "inurement" of the church's Income and could affect the church's tax-exempt status.

If the church provides its minister with an automobile, the use of that automobile must be valued and reported as compensation. There are four valuation methods and one of the four must be utilized. These methods are the General Valuation Principle, Special Automobile Lease Valuation Rule, Special Cents-Per-Mile Rule, and Special Commuting Valuation Rule.

1. **General Valuation Principle** - With this method, the amount to include as compensation is determined by taking the amount an individual would have to pay to lease a comparable vehicle on comparable terms in the same geographical and multiplying it by

the percentage of total vehicle miles for the period that were of a personal nature rather than of a business one.

2. **Special Automobile Lease Valuation Rule** - With this method, the amount to include as compensation is determined by taking the amount of the annual lease value of the automobile and multiplying it by the percentage of total miles driven during the year that are for personal use.
3. **Special Cents-Per Mile Rule** - With this method, the amount to include as compensation is determined by taking the actual miles driven for personal use and multiplying it by the Internal Revenue Service standard mileage rate.
4. **Special Commuting Valuation Rule** - With this method, the amount to include as compensation is computed with a rate of $3.00 per round-trip commute or $1.50 per one-way commute (commuting miles are always deemed personal miles). For this rule to apply, the following conditions must be met:

1. The vehicle must be owned or leased by the church,
2 For non-compensatory business reasons, it is a requirement of the church that the employee commutes to and from work,
3. With a written policy statement in place by the church board, the vehicle cannot be used for personal reasons except for commuting or minimal personal use such as lunch stops between business trips,
    1. There is a reasonable believe by the church that the vehicle is not used for personal use,

2. The employee who is required to commute to work is not a board appointed, confirmed, or elected officer whose annual compensation is $70,000 or more, a director, or an employee with an annual compensation of $145,000 or more,
3. There is sufficient evidence, by the church, to prove the preceding five conditions.

TAX FORMS FORM W-2 AND FORM 1099 MISC.

For income tax purposes, the wages received by a minister should be reported on the Form W -2 by the church. In Box 1 of this form, all cash income from the church such as salary, auto allowances, convention expenses, any social security paid by the church on behalf of the minister, any cash gifts from the church such as at Christmas, and the fair market value of gifts such as cars, love offerings or the value of any forgiven debts. However, Box 1 should not include the minister's housing allowance or fair market rental value nor should it contain any utility allowances. These monies should be reported separately in Box 14 of the Form W2. Boxes 2, 4, and 6, Federal Income tax withheld, social security tax withheld, and Medicare tax withheld should all be blank, unless the minister voluntarily authorized the church to withhold an estimated amount for each out of each pay period.

If the minister does authorize the additional withholding, Box 2 will reflect the total amount withheld. Boxes 4 and 6, social security tax withheld and Medicare tax withheld should remain blank, as should Box 3, for Social Security wages and box 5, for Medicare wages. **In** addition to Form W-2, Form 1099 Misc. should be used when a church pays a visiting minister or someone other that an employee of the church for services such as revivals, seminars, conferences, etc. Box 7, Non-employee Compensation, should reflect what the church paid for the services rendered.

FORM 1040, U.S. INDIVIDUAL INCOME TAX RETURN

The compensation received by ministers, as shown in Box 1 of Form W-2 should be reported on Line 7, Wages, Salaries, Tips, etc. of the Form 1040. The amount of the excess housing and utility allowances over a minister's actual cost of these items should be reported on Line 22, the Other Income line of Form 1040. It is important here to reemphasize that a minister's housing and utility allowance should be approved, in writing, in advance by the church. It should not be determined at a later date.

SCHEDULE A, ITEMIZED DEDUCTIONS

For a minister's itemized deductions, such as medical and dental expenses, state income taxes, taxes (Personal Property), interest (Mortgage), contributions, casualty and thefts losses, and un-reimbursed business expenses (Form 2106), Schedule A is used. This form is attached to the Form 1040. Property taxes, mortgage interest, un-reimbursed business expenses, and contributions are areas of immediate interest for a minister. The Tax Reform Act of 1989 - Public Law 99-514, provided that a minister receiving excludable parsonage and housing allowances can deduct real property taxes and mortgage interest on his or her residence.

Un-reimbursed business expense deductions such as office supplies, materials, postage, entertainment, education expenses, and depreciation on the cost of office furniture and fixtures purchased by the minister can and should be deducted in the section Miscellaneous Deductions, starting on Line 20 of Schedule A. For educational expenses, the deductible expenditures are those that maintain or improve ministerial skills.

SCHEDULE C, PROFIT OR LOSS FROM BUSINESS OR PROFESSION

Other than wages or salary, a minister's income such as compensation from weddings, funerals, revivals, or other such church related activities should be reported on Schedule C. Part 1. **In** addition, any expenses directly related to this income should be deducted on this form as well. Examples of a few of these expenses are booklets for marriage or family and mileage (automobile) along with other related expenses. Any other income a minister has that is not related to his or her church ministry should be reported on the appropriate line of page one of Form 1040 accompanied by the appropriate schedule of form if required.

HOME (BUSINESS USE OF HOME)

For ministers who have income from self-employment activities and utilize the Form Schedule C, to deduct expenses for the use of your home in your business, a part of your home must be used regularly and exclusively as:

1. The principal place of business for any trade or business in which you engage; or
2. The place where you meet and deal with your patients, clients, or

customers in the normal course of your trade or business; or

3. In connection with your trade or business, if you use a separate structure that is not attached to your home.

The amount you are allowed to deduct is based upon the percentage of your home you utilize for business. To compute the percentage, you can divide the number of square feet used for business by the total square footage of your home. Or, if the rooms are very close in size, divide the number of rooms used for business by the total number of rooms in your home. From this point, the business expense portion can be computed by multiplying the percentage by the total of each expense.

If you are utilizing both your home and another location regularly for business, you must decide which location is your principal place of business. To make this determination, there are two primary factors. One factor is the amount of time spent at each location and the second factor is the relative importance of the activities you performed at each location.

You cannot deduct the cost of lawn care maintenance for your home as a business expense; however, you can include as business expenses the business portion of mortgage interest, real estate taxes, utilities, depreciation, insurance, painting and repair for the portion utilized for business, rent and casualty losses.

SCHEDULE SE, COMPUTATION OF SOCIAL SECURITY SELF-EMPLOYMENT TAX

Both the minister's salary reported on Line 7 of Form 1040 and the net profit from Schedule C are considered to be self-employment income for social security purposes. Also, this is the one place the minister's housing allowance or the fair rental value of the parsonage provided and the utility allowance are reported. The total amount reported on Line 2 of Form SE is calculated by adding the figures in Box 1 of Form W-2, Box 14 of Form W-2, and the net profit from the Schedule C.

Once this amount has been calculated, reduce it by the amount of the business expenses reported on Form 2106 and the un-reimbursed business expenses itemized on Schedule A related to the church business. Finally, once you have calculated the total self-employment income for Line 2 of Schedule SE, the self-employment tax is computed on Schedule SE and carried forward to page 2 of the Form 1040, Line 48.

FORM 2106, EMPLOYEE BUSINESS EXPENSES

Form 2106 is used to record un-reimbursed employee business related expenses such as travel, transportation, and educational expenses unless you have already deducted them on Schedule C. The travel expense deduction for the business use of a minister's automobile and a minister's un-reimbursed meals and lodging while away from home overnight on business are a few of the primary expenses for ministers entered on this form.

WITHHOLDING TAXES

As a self-employed individual for social security purposes, ministers are required to pay their taxes quarterly in the form of *estimated taxes payments* during or at the end of each quarter *(lst Quarter=Jan, Feb, Mar; 2nd Quarter=Apr, May, Jun; 3rd Quarter Jul, Aug, Sep; 4th Quarter=Oct, Nov, Dee).* Due to the fact that ministers are self-employed for social security tax purposes, they cannot withhold payroll taxes on themselves. The estimated tax payments should be submitted along with the Form 1040ES (Federal) and along with whatever state form is required by the state in which the minister is licensed, commissioned, or ordained. If the quarterly estimated tax payments are not made, a minister will not only find him or herself facing a large income tax liability at tax time, the Internal Revenue

Service could also penalize the minister for under estimating his or her income tax liability. Since there is no employer to match the social security (FICA and MEDICARE) tax, ministers are required to pay the entire amount themselves in the form of a self-employment tax.

A minister who reports his or her income as an employee does have the option of allowing the church to perform "voluntary withholding" of his or her federal income taxes. Under the voluntary withholding arrangement, the minister gives his or her consent for the church to withhold a certain amount of federal income taxes from his or her wages. The church is only obligated to withhold the minister's federal income tax liability and is not required to match any of the withholdings. The amount withheld from the minister's wages can constitutes the minister's quarterly estimated tax payment.

THE CHURCH FREEDOM OF RELIGION

The United States Constitution guarantees freedom of religion. Article VII, Amendment 1 [1791] of the Constitution states, "Congress **shall make no law respecting an establishment of religion or prohibiting the free** exercise **thereof."** Therefore, Congress is required to leave churches alone so that an individual(s) can serve and worship God in any way they choose without the restriction of its activities. In addition to not restricting the activities of the church, Congress also cannot establish a state religion or any guidelines governing the church. Although the phrase "separation of church and state" is not written in the Constitution, it was adopted by Congress to show that they are not involved in the church's affairs by creating governmental guidelines. However, the Constitution does state and require the involvement of Congress to insure the protection of religious freedom.

Churches and their affiliated agencies have been excluded from federal and state taxation requirements. If a church were not tax exempt, this would give Congress the ability to create guidelines and regulations governing the church. This action could in all possibility lead to the destruction of the church body as we know and see it. Because of this possibility, the church has and still is be exempt from federal and state taxation requirements. However, although the church is exempt from federal and state taxation requirements, it is not exempt from having to pay payroll taxes and file payroll reports. In this respect, the church is treated just as any other business. The above paragraphs on "Freedom of Religion" highlight why "The Clergy Housing Clarification Act of 2002" ruling was so important.

DEFINITION OF A CHURCH

The proper definition of a church is very important. Because churches are exempt from the requirements to file for determination and recognition of exempt status, the Internal Revenue Service must rule on what is a church. The American Heritage Dictionary, Second College Edition has over eight definitions of a church. Listed here are just a few.

1. The company of all Christians regarded as a mystic spiritual body.
2. A building for public, esp. Christians, worship.
3. Ecclesiastical power as distinguished from the secular: the separation of church and state.
4. Christian Science. "The structure of Truth and Love."

As stated earlier, these are just a few of the definitions listed to define a church. As one can see, it is nearly impossible for Congress to single out one definition of a church.

DETERMINING CHURCH STATUS

Many organizations try to take advantage of the protection under the status of being a church. Cult organizations, hate groups, and organizations that are set-up for illegal purposes are a few entities that try to take advantage of having a church status. Because the Internal Revenue Code does not state anyone definition of a church, the Internal Revenue Service has set guidelines for determining what is a church.

1. **Legal Existence:** A church must have a definite legal existence. This can be achieved with Articles of Incorporation filed with the state the church was founded in.
2. **An Ecclesiastical Government:** The church must have a form of government set forth. This can be achieved with by-laws.
3. A **Statement of Faith:** The church must have a creed of worship or a statement of faith. This can be achieved within the by-laws or a separate written document.
4. **Church History:** The church's history is very important and should be written and updated annually.
5. **Established Place** of Worship: The church must have an established place for worship service. This place may be a temporary facility as long as the congregation knows what services will be held and when.
6. **Regular Scheduled Services:** The church must have and state regular times for services.
7. **Membership Not Associated with Another Church:** The church should maintain a record system of keeping membership records as well as a system of transferring the membership of new members coming from another church to join the new church.
8. **Regular Congregation:** The church must maintain a list of regular members that attend the church.

9. **School/Training Programs:** A church should have Sunday Schools, Ministerial Preparation Schools and other training schools to teach members of the church about the church's beliefs and history.
10. **Ministerial Preparation and Ordaining:** The church should have a written prescribed course of study for ordained ministers and lay workers. The course should give credibility to ministerial credentials.
11. **Open to the Public:** The church service must be open to the public.

Although the total number of criteria has not been specified for determining a church status, the eleven (11) listed above are mainly what the Internal Revenue Service uses when determining the status of a church. Also, the eleven (11) criteria listed above are from questions asked on the Form 1023 (Application for Recognition of Exemption).

DETERMINING THE TAX-EXEMPT STATUS OF THE CHURCH

In 1986, the United States adopted into law the Tax Reform Act. The Internal Revenue Service now refers to this as the Internal Revenue Code of 1986. The Tax Reform Act was designed for the Internal

Revenue Service to better collect taxes from individuals, groups, and companies. It also provided tax credits and tax deductions to donors of tax exempt organizations. The Federal Government is seeking to verify the tax-exempt status of all not-for-profit organizations by requiring certain documents to be maintained by the organization.

The Internal Revenue Service has established six (6) conditions that address not-for-profit organizations including churches under the IRC 5 0 1 c 3 Codes. They are:

1. The organization must be incorporated or have some form of legal status.
2. The organization is organized exclusively for exempt purposes.
3. The organization is operated exclusively for exempt purposes.
4. The organization does not engage in substantial efforts to influence legislation.
5. The organization does not participate to any extent in a political campaign for or against any candidate for public office.
6. None of the organization's assets can be used to benefit private individuals.

Paragraph 508 of the Revenue Code, enacted with the Tax Reform

Act of 1969, defines the types of organizations that are eligible for exemption of federal income taxes. Also, this section states that all such organizations must seek Internal Revenue Service determination of exempt status before being considered exempt under paragraph 501(c)(3). An application Form 1023 (Application for Recognition of Exemption) must be filed for consideration of exempt status. However, under the heading of **Mandatory Exceptions,** the code states that churches, their integrated auxiliaries, and conventions or associations of churches are **exempt** from the requirements of having to file for determination and recognition of exempt status. This means that churches are already 501(c)(3) organizations. **Churches do not have to file Form 1023 requesting tax-exempt determination** is printed on the Form 1023.

However, the church may find it to its advantage to obtain recognition of exemption. In doing so, the church should submit information showing that it is a church, a religious order, or a religious organization that is an integral part of a church and is operating within the functions of a church.

RELIGION AND POLITICS

It is imperative that ministers and churches abide by the Internal Revenue Service regulations prohibiting them from participating in partisan politics. This prohibition only concerns races for public office, and not issues. Ministers are permitted to speak on moral and political issues. These issues include, but are not limited to issues such as abortion rights, gay rights, gun control, healthcare, and ballot referendums. This is the case even if the minister is speaking on these issues from the pulpit, or within some other type of forum. However, neither churches nor ministers may endorse a particular candidate, or advise congregants to vote for or against a particular candidate. The federal income tax laws that govern such behavior are very strict, and the Internal Revenue Service has indicated it adheres to a "zero tolerance" policy in regards to violations.

The types of activities ministers and churches are not permitted to engage in under the Internal Revenue Service code are very specific. Ministers and churches are strictly prohibited from endorsing candidates, or generating statements in favor of or in opposition towards candidates. The acts that constitute an endorsement or opposition of a candidate include, but are not limited to letters of endorsement or opposition that have been printed on the church's letterhead, distribution of campaign literature that is sponsored by the church, ministers advising their congregants who to vote for or not to vote for from the pulpit, and allowing candidates to display their campaign signs on the property of the church. These restrictions do not prevent ministers from endorsing candidates as individuals outside the church, or during the minister's personal time. Churches are also not allowed to contribute or solicit contributions on a candidate's behalf. Nor is the church permitted to donate funds to a candidate's political campaign. Violation penalties can range from financial penalties imposed on the church and church officials to the loss of the church's tax -exempt status.

Although there are many things that are not permissible by ministers and churches in reference to politics, there are quite a few things ministers and churches are permitted to do in reference to politics. For example, churches are permitted to sponsor voter registration drives, churches can encourage voter participation, and churches can even go as far as to assist individuals with getting to the polls on election-day. Churches are even permitted to sponsor non-partisan forums for the candidates. Of course the types of questions presented should be of a non-partisan nature, and cover a broad range of issues, and not just moral or social issues that are of concern to the church. If they desire, a church is permitted to send questionnaires to candidates asking them where they stand on issues. However, be mindful that the church should make sure that the responses from the candidates are accurate, and that the questionnaire covers a broad range of issues before they distribute the responses. The church should sent questionnaires to each candidate, and the candidate's responses should not be compared to the preferred position of the church on the issue.

THE INTERNAL REVENUE SERVICE REVOKES A CHURCH'S TAX-EXEMPT STATUS

The Internal Revenue Service can and did revoke the tax -exempt status of a church because of its involvement in political activities. In 1995, the Internal Revenue Service revoked the tax-exempt status of Branch Ministries, Inc. for intervening in a political campaign. For churches and other religious organizations, to maintain their tax-exempt status, they must comply with requirements specified in section 501(c)(3) of the income tax code. One such requirement is that the church or religious organization cannot intervene or participate in any political campaign on behalf of or against any person running for a public office. In this particular case, the church published full-page ads in two national newspapers urging Christians not to vote for Bill Clinton during the 1992 presidential election. A federal court, in 1999, upheld the Internal Revenue Service decision and rejected the claim made by the church that its first amendment, the Religious Freedom Act, and the Church Audit Procedures Act were violated. *Branch Ministries, Inc.* v. *Commissioner, 40 F Supp.2d* 15 *(D.D.C. 1999)*

The reclassification of a church or religious organization from a tax-exempt entity to a taxable entity could be financially devastating. Being familiar with and operating within the guidelines of section 5 0

1 c 3 is not an option. It's a requirement.

INTEGRATED AUXILIARIES

The Internal Revenue Code makes reference to **Integrated Auxiliaries** of a church being included under the church's exempt status. Although there is no term specifically defining an integrated auxiliary in the tax code, a church auxiliary is considered a principle activity of the church. An integrated auxiliary can be in the form of daycare services, nursing homes, soup kitchens, and youth groups, etc. The auxiliaries are exempt from taxes just as the church is as long as it is operated by the church and under the same Employer Identification Number.

THE CHURCH & EMPLOYEES

Churches are not exempt from paying payroll taxes. Both the Internal Revenue Service and the Courts have rejected the argument that the paying of payroll taxes infringes upon the church's constitutional guaranty of religious freedom. However, in 1984, the Federal Government did allow churches that had non-minister employees as of July of 1984 to exempt themselves from the employer's share of the FICA and Medicare taxes. **In** order to be granted exemption, the church had to file a timely Form 8274 with the Internal Revenue

Service by October 30, 1984. Although this sounded like a good idea and many churches applied for the exemption, the other side of the coin was church employees had to file their taxes as self-employed for social security purposes. That means those employees had to pay their own self-employment tax just like the minister.

As stated earlier, churches are not excluded from federal income taxes if it pays wages to employees it is responsible for withholding, depositing, paying, and reporting federal income taxes and social security taxes (FICA and Medicare) on those wages on the appropriate forms by the appropriate time. This rule also applies to the withholding of state taxes from the employees' wages.

It is important to remember, the church has the liability of matching the FICA and Medicare taxes withheld from the employees' wages. In addition to making deposits, the church also has to file quarterly reports to report payroll taxes withheld. The church, if it has employees, should receive payroll tax withholding booklets on both the federal and state.

REPORTING REQUIREMENTS FOR CHURCHES

There are ten common reporting requirements that apply to churches. They are:

1. Obtaining an Employer Identification Number,

2. Determining the status of a worker and obtaining each worker's social security number,
3. Insuring they have a completed W4 (Withholding Allowance Certificate) from each worker,
4. Calculating the amount of each employee's wages (this includes other taxable items as well as any fringe benefits),
5. Determining the amount of federal income taxes to be withheld from an employee's wages,
6. Withholding the appropriate amount of FICA taxes from employees' wages,
7. Making the appropriate payroll tax deposits with their bank if the withheld payroll taxes exceed $500.00 at the end of the month,
8. Submitting a completed “nine-forty-one” (Employer's Quarterly Tax Return) with the Internal Revenue Service at the end of the quarter,
9. Issuing W-2s by February 1st of the following year to every employee and forwarding copies of all W 2s to the Social Security Administration before March 1st of the following year with the appropriate W3 transmittal form,
10. Issuing a 1099-MISC to any non-employee worker or contractor who was paid $600.00 or more for the year by February 1st of the following year and forwarding a copy of all 1099- MISC forms to the Internal Revenue Service before March 1st of the following year with the appropriate 1096

transmittal form.

It is very important that church leaders take these rules very seriously. There are penalties imposed for noncompliance and church officers may be personally responsible and liable for these penalties. These penalties can equal the amount of the payroll taxes that are not withheld or deposited. Section 6672 of the Internal Revenue Code simply states that any corporate officer, director, or employee who **is** responsible for withholding and depositing payroll taxes is liable for 100% of these taxes if they are not withheld or not paid to the government. And yes, the penalty imposed by section 6672 of the Internal Revenue Code does apply to churches as well as other non-profit organizations.

EMPLOYER IDENTIFICATION NUMBER

If the church has employees and is required to give tax statements, or is required to report employment taxes, it needs an employer identification number. The employer identification number is a nine-digit number issued by the IRS. The number is very much similar in use to a social security number. The IRS to identify a business utilizes it. Just as no two people have the same social security number, no two businesses have the same employer identification number. The Form SS-4 is the form submitted to the IRS to request an employer identification number. A business should have only one

EIN number. If you take over another business, do not use the original EIN. Apply for a different number. One of the questions you will encounter while preparing the Form SS-4 is what type of organizational structure is your organization.

WHO IS AN EMPLOYEE

In general, churches are required to withhold income taxes, and withhold and pay social security and Medicare taxes on wages paid to its employee or employees. If an individual is classified as an independent contractor and during an audit, the Internal Revenue Services deems the individual an employee and reclassifies the individual as an employee, the church will become liable for all payroll taxes that were not withheld and paid plus whatever penalties and interest are appropriate. Therefore, it is very important that the minister and church officials understand what the Internal Revenue Service looks at when determining the employment status of an individual.

In general, an individual who performs services for the church is considered an employee of the church if the church can control what will be done, and the method in which it will be done. This is the case even if the individual is given freedom of action. In other words, the church need not exercise control over the manner in which the work is performed, the mere fact that the church has the right to control the employee when it is appropriate and deemed necessary is all that is required to meet the qualification of control. It is extremely important that the absence of the need to control the manner in which the individual performs his or her duties is not confused with the absence of the **right** to control.

There are at least four tests that are utilized to determine the status of an individual. They include: The "common law employee" test, The "20 factor" test, The "7 factor" test, and The" 12 factor" test.

The "common law employee" test is one of the most frequently used tests by the **IRS** and the tax courts. This test basically deals with the issue of the right-to-control in reference to the employer-employee relationship.

The IRS "20 factor" test was developed "as an aid in determining whether an individual is an employee under the common law rules," *Revenue Ruling* 87-41. The 20 factors are as follows:

1. Instructions - An individual who has to comply with instructions about when, where, and how to work is ordinarily an employee.
2. Training - Training of an individual by an experienced employee or by other means is a factor of control and indicates an employee status.
3. Integration - Integration of an individual's services into the

business operations generally displays that the individual is subject to direction and control and is therefore an employee.

4. Services Rendered Personally - If the services must be provided by the individual personally, it may suggests an employer-employee relationship. Normally when an individual is self-employed, he or she has the right to hire a substitute without the employer's knowledge.
5. Hiring, supervising, and paying assistants - Hiring, supervising, and payment of assistants by an employer normally indicates that the workers on the job are employees.
6. Continuing relationship - If after the individual has performed the required services the existence of a continuing relationship between the individual and the company or organization develops, this may indicate an employer-employee relationship.
7. Set hours of work - The establishment of set hours to work by the employer is an indication of an employer-employee relationship.
8. Full time required - If the employer establishes the worker must devote full time to the business, the worker is ordinarily an employee.
9. Performing the work on the employer's premises - Performing the job on the employer's premises may indicate an employee status especially if the work can be performed somewhere else.
10. Order or sequence of work - If the employer controls the sequence or order of the work being performed, this indicates employee status.

11. Oral or written report - If the employer requires the worker to submit written or oral reports regularly, an employer-employee relationship may exist.
12. Payment by hour, week, or month - Employees are normally paid by the hour, week, or month.
13. Payment of business expenses - If the employer pays the worker's business or travel expenses, an employer-employee relationship may exist.
14. Furnishing of tools and materials - When an employer furnishes the tools and materials, this indicates an employer-employee relationship.
15. Significant Investment- The employer furnishing all the necessary equipment and premises displays an employer-employee relationship.
16. Realization of profit or loss - Not being in a position to realize a profit or a loss indicates an employee status.
17. Working for more than one firm at a time - A self-employed individual usually works for more that one firm at a time.
18. Making services available to the general public - Normally, individuals who offer their services to the general public are self-employed.
19. Right to discharge - An employer normally cannot fire a self-employed individual as long as the work is being performed based upon the contractual agreement.
20. Right to terminate - Ordinarily an employee can terminate the

relationship with an employer at any time without incurring liability.

<u>The Tax Court's "7 factor" test</u> factors are as follows:

1. The degree of employer control over the worker,
2. Which party invests in the facilities utilized to perform the work,
3. The opportunity for profit or loss for the worker,
4. Whether the employer has the right to discharge the worker,
5. Whether the work being performed is a part of the employer's regular business,
6. The permanency of the relationship that exists between the employer and the worker,
7. The relationship the employer and worker believe they are creating.

<u>The Supreme Court's "12 factor" test</u> factors are as follows:

1. The employer's rights in regards to controlling the manner in which the job will be performed and completed,
2. The source providing the tools and supplies that will be utilized to complete the work,
3. The location from which the work will be performed,
4. The duration of the relationship between the employer and the worker,
5. The employer's right to assign additional projects to the worker,
6. The employer's control in regards to the amount of time it will take

the worker to complete the job,

7. The payment method,
8. The employer's role in regards to hiring the worker,
9. The employer's role in regards to paying the worker,
10. Whether the work being performed is a part of the regular business of the employer,
11. Whether the employer in business,
12. The benefits the worker receives.

RECLASSIFICA TION

If an individual is classified as an independent contractor and during an audit, the Internal Revenue Services deems the individual an employee and reclassifies the individual as an employee, the church will become liable for all payroll taxes that were not withheld and paid plus whatever penalties and interest are appropriate. Therefore, it is very important that the minister and church officials understand what the Internal Revenue Service looks at when determining the employment status of an individual.

In general, an individual who performs services for the church is considered an employee of the church if the church can control what will be done, and the method in which it will be done. This is the case even if the individual is given freedom of action. In other words, the church need not exercise control over the manner in which the work is performed, the mere fact that the church has the right to control the employee when it is appropriate and deemed necessary is all that is required to meet the qualification of control. It is extremely important that the absence of the need to control the manner in which the individual performs his or her duties is not confused with the absence of the **right** to control.

INDEPENDENT CONTRACTOR

An independent contractor is anyone who provides a service to others outside the boundaries of an employee. Churches need to be very careful because the Internal Revenue Service can be very aggressive in its attempt to reclassify a worker as an employee. It is not uncommon for organizations to label an individual as an independent contractor in order to avoid paying payroll taxes. It is very important to understand the rules, and the criteria the Internal Revenue Service utilizes when determining if an individual is an employee or not. To prove independent contractor status, it must be proven the independent contractor has the right to control the manner in which the work is to be accomplished. **In** other words, the issue of whether or not the independent contractor is under someone else's control in regards to the work environment becomes an issue. It is also quite beneficial for the church and the independent contractor if the independent contractor furnishes his or her own supplies and/or equipment based upon the type of work being performed. A written contract would also be very instrumental if there is ever a discrepancy.

BACKUP WITHHOLDINGS

It is extremely important for churches and their financial bodies to realize that if an independent contractor performs services and is paid at least $600.00 for the year, if that independent contractor is not a corporation, a taxpayer identification number should be furnished by the contractor and a Form 1099 issued to the contractor by the church. If the independent contractor fails to furnish the church with a taxpayer identification number (Federal **ID** or Social Security Number), the church is required by law to withhold 31 % of the amount of the compensation as "backup withholding." This should be done at the time of payment. After the payment has been made is too late.

WAGES AND PAYROLL

Employees bring about a whole new set of responsibilities and liabilities not to mention expenses. Properly withholding, depositing, and reporting payroll taxes are of the utmost importance. Churches have been penalized by the Internal Revenue Service for not properly withholding, depositing, and reporting payroll taxes. The following information will take the guesswork out of the responsibilities of properly withholding, depositing, and reporting payroll taxes.

PAYROLL REPORTS AND FORMS

There are a number of payroll reports and forms churches are responsible for submitting. By the end of the month following the end of the quarter ***(lst Quarter = Jan, Feb, Mar: Due Date = Apr. 30; 2nd Quarter = Apr, May, Jun: Due Date July* 31; *3rd Quarter = Jul, Aug, Sep: Due Date = Oct.* 31; *4th Quarter = Oct, Nov, Dec: Due Date Jan.* 31)** churches are required to submit a Form “nine-forty-one” (Employer's Quarterly Federal Tax Return). The Form “nine-forty-one” reports all federal income taxes, social security, and Medicare taxes withheld and/or deposited during the quarter. This form is automatically sent to the church from the Internal Revenue Service. The Internal Revenue Service becomes aware of the church's status by the submission of the Form SS-4, and other pertinent paperwork filed by the church. If the church has an employee or employees and has not received its preprinted Form 941 via the mail, contact the Internal Revenue Service immediately. The number for the Internal Revenue Service is 1-800-829-1040.

PAYROLL TAX DEPOSITS

Churches must deposit federal income taxes withheld, state income taxes withheld where applicable, the employee social security and Medicare taxes, and the employer's matching funds for the social security and Medicare taxes. Payroll tax deposits are made by depositing the appropriate funds at a financial institution that is an authorized depository for Federal taxes. If you are unsure, ask your banker if the institution is an authorized depository for Federal taxes. The deposits are made using the Form 8109 Federal Tax Deposit Coupon. New employers usually receive their coupon book from the Internal Revenue Service within 5 to 6 weeks after receiving an employer identification number. If your church has not received its preprinted Form 81 09s by the time it is required to make its first deposit, a Form 8109-B, which is an over-the-counter version of the Form 8109, can be utilized. However, by no means should deposits be made at an authorized depository if you have not received your employer identification number from the Internal Revenue Service. Without an employer identification number, the payment should be made payable to the "United States Treasury" and write on it the church's name (as shown on the SS-4), address, kind of tax, period covered, and the date the church's employer identification number was applied for. Do not use the Form 8109-B in this situation.

There are taxpayers that are required to electronically deposit their tax payments by using the Electronic Federal Tax Deposit System (E F T P S) in 2002. These taxpayers are identified by two factors:

1. If the total tax deposits of such taxes in 2000 were more than $200,000 or
2. If the taxpayer was required to use EFTPS in 2001.

If you are not required to deposit electronically, you can volunteer to do so. To receive more information, or to enroll in EFTPS, call 1-800-555-4477 or 1-800945-8400.

It is very important that deposits are made timely. Churches are required to deposit 100% of the tax liability on or before the deposit due date (Accuracy of Deposit Rule). However, if a church fails to deposit less than 100%, no penalty will be accessed if the following 2 conditions are met:

1. Any deposit shortfall does not exceed the greater of $100 or 2% of the amount of taxes otherwise required to be deposited and
2. The deposit shortfall is paid or deposited by the shortfall date as described below.

Makeup Date for Deposit Shortfall

1. **Monthly schedule depositor.** Deposit the shortfall or pay it with your return by the due date of the Form “nine-forty-one” for the quarter in which the shortfall occurred. You may pay the shortfall

with Form "nine-forty-one" even if the amount is $2,500 or more.

2. **Semiweekly schedule depositor.** Deposit by the earlier of:

1. The first Wednesday or Friday that falls on or after the 15th of the month following the month in which the shortfall occurred or
2. The due date of Form "nine-forty-one" (for the quarter of the tax liability).

Your payment may be made along with the Form "nine-forty-one" if:

1. You accumulate less than a $2,500 tax liability during the quarter, and you pay in full with a time filed "nine-forty-one" return.
2. You are a monthly scheduled depositor and make a payment in accordance with the Accuracy of Deposits Rule.

Monthly Depositor:

You are considered a monthly depositor for a calendar year if the total taxes on your Form "nine-forty-one" (line 11) for the four quarters in your look back period totaled $50,000 or less. As a monthly depositor, your payroll tax deposits have to be made by the 15th day of the next month. For example, when the month ends on January 31, the tax deposit has to be made no later than by February 15th. **(Note: The look back is a four-quarter period that begins on July 1 and ends on Jun 30.)**

Semiweekly Depositor:

You are considered a semiweekly depositor for a calendar year if the total taxes on your Form "nine-forty-one" (line 11) for the four quarters in your look back period totaled more than $50,000. As a semiweekly depositor, your payroll tax deposits have to be made by the following Wednesday if the payday falls on a Wednesday, Thursday, and/or Friday, and by the following Friday if the payday falls on a Saturday, Sunday, Monday, and/or Tuesday. **(Note: The look back is a four-quarter period that begins on July 1 and ends on Jun 30.)**

$100.000 Next-Day Deposit Rule:

If you accumulate a tax liability of (reduced by any advanced Earned Income Payments) $100,000 or more during a deposit period, your payroll tax deposit must be made the next banking day regardless of whether you are a monthly or semiweekly depositor.

Penalties may apply if the required deposits are not made on time. If the failure to make a proper and timely deposit was due to a reasonable cause and not willful neglect, the penalties will not apply. The penalty rates for not making deposits timely or properly are:

1. 2% - Deposits made 1 to 5 days late.
2. 5% - Deposits made 6 to 15 days late.
3. 10% - Deposits made 16 or more days late. Also applies to amounts paid within 10 days of the date of the first notice the Internal Revenue Service send asking for the tax due.

4. 10% - Deposits made at an unauthorized financial institution, paid directly to the Internal Revenue Service, or paid with your tax return.
5. 10% - Amounts subject to electronic deposit requirements but not deposited using EFTPS.
6. 15% - Amounts still unpaid more than 10 days after the date of the first notice the Internal Revenue Service sent asking for the tax due or the day on which you receive notice and demand for immediate payment, whichever is earlier.

EMPLOYEES OF 501(c)(3) ORGANIZATIONS

Nonprofit organizations that are exempt from income tax under section 501(c)(3) of the Internal Revenue Code include any community chest, fund, or foundation organized and operated exclusively for religious, charitable, scientific, testing for public safety, literary or educational purposes, fostering national or international amateur sports competition, or for the prevention of cruelty to children or animals. These organizations are usually corporations and are exempt from income tax under section 501 (a).

Wages paid to employees of section 501(c)(3) organizations are subject to social security and Medicare taxes unless one of the following situations applies:

1. The organization pays an employee less than $100 in a calendar year.
2. The organization is a church or church-controlled organization opposed for religious reasons to the payment of social security and Medicare taxes and has filed **Form 8274,** Certification by Churches and Qualified Church Controlled Organizations Electing Exemption From Employer Social Security and Medicare Taxes, to elect exemption from social security and Medicare taxes. The organization must have filed for exemption before the first date on which a quarterly employment tax return (Form 941) would otherwise be due.

An employee of a church or church-controlled organization that is exempt from social security and Medicare taxes must pay self-employment tax if the employee is paid $108.28 or more in a year. However, an employee who is a member of a qualified religious sect can apply for an exemption from the self-employment tax by filing **Form 4029,** Application for Exemption From Social Security and Medicare Taxes and Waiver of Benefits. See **Members of recognized religious sects opposed to insurance** in section 4. An organization that is exempt from income tax under section 50lc3 of the Internal Revenue Code is also exempt from the Federal unemployment (FUTA) tax. This exemption cannot be waived.

CHURCH GOVERNMENT

Although many definitions of the term "Government" exists, we will define the term "Government" as the act or process of governing, esp. the control and administration of public policy (The American Heritage Dictionary, Second College Edition). Every church must have some type of formal governing system for internal control. Because of tradition, some elders of a church set rules and regulations based on what worked in the past and what has been handed down over the years. Then again, some of the larger denominational churches have their governing procedures written and published. It does not matter how large or how small a church is, a good system of governing is essential.

The lack of a good governing system could be looked upon as the church operating for personal gain and since the Internal Revenue Service looks at the governing of a church when determining tax-exempt status, a solid system of governing is a must. If the Internal Revenue Service audits a church and finds no formal form of governing, the Internal Revenue Service can and may disallow or revoke the tax-exempt status of the church. A good place to start reviewing the church's governmental policies is with the Mission Statement. The Articles and by-laws of the church may also prove helpful in the organization of the church's governing system.

ACCOUNTING PROCEDURES FOR THE CHURCH

Revenue (Income) received by the church and Expenditures (Expenses) paid out by the church must be monitored and recorded through every phase of processing. This is very important because one of the main criteria for tax-exempt status is that the funds not be utilized for personal gain. Developing an internal control and record keeping system for the monitoring and documentation of the utilization of church funds with more than one person in control is as important as the church's governing system. Having only one person in charge of the monies received by and paid out by the church can and have resulted in possible embezzlement of church funds leaving the church and the organizing body liable.

Monies collected should be counted and recorded on paper and signed by all members of the finance committee. A record of contributions made by cash and checks should be listed separately. A duplicate deposit slip should be made at the time of the final count of the monies received before leaving the church and once deposited, the duplicate deposit slip should be attached to the original deposit slip. A written collection and disbursement policy regarding the governing and the handling of all monies received by the church should be adopted as well as a check and balance system. For example, no one person should be in charge of collections, deposits, disbursements, and accounts maintained. There should be a team to collect the monies received by the church, if possible, two signers of checks for the church, and an internal auditor to reconcile the book(s). **In** addition, the church should have an outside auditor or certified public accountant examine the books on an annual basis. Because of the many auxiliaries of the church, policies regarding their handling of funds collected should be in place. For example, after each auxiliary function, a written report should be given to the church's treasurer. There should be at least three checking accounts for the church and all funds should be deposited into the appropriate accounts. No money should be taken home by the members or kept in any individual personal account.

A budget is also a very important part of the church's accounting system. A budget shows how the church plans to disburse the funds collected and the amount of funds needed to complete its financial goals. A budget will help the church maintain its monthly obligations.

REIMBURSEMENT PLANS

There are two types of reimbursement plans I want to bring to your attention. One is an Accountable Plan and the other is a Non-accountable plan. The Accountable plan requires the employee to meet all three of the following rules:

1. The employee must have paid or incurred deductible expenses while performing services as your employee.
2. The employee must adequately account to you for these expenses within a reasonable period of time.
3. The employee must return any amounts in excess of expenses within a reasonable period of time.

Under a non-accountable plan, payments to an employee for travel or necessary business expenses are treated as wages, and are subject to income, social securing, Medicare, and other appropriate tax withholdings. Payments are treated as paid under a non-accountable plan if:

1. The employee is not required to or does not substantiate timely those expenses to you with receipts or other documentation or
2. You advance an amount to an employee for business expenses and the employee is not require to or does not return timely any amount he or she does not use for business expenses.

Establishing an Accountable reimbursement plan would be the best route to take for your church. Under this plan, all reimbursed expenses are not reported as income. These reimbursed expenses include, but are not limited to: office supplies, religious material, dues and subscriptions, meals and entertainment, seminars and memberships, educational expenses, camps, legal and professional services, automobile expenses, etc.

AUDITING OF A CHURCH

The Internal Revenue Code, Paragraph 7602 gives the Internal Revenue Service authority to conduct audits of persons or organizations to:

1. Determine the correct amount of taxable income if any,
2. Make a return where none has been filed,
3. Determine the liability of any person or organization for any federal tax, and
4. To collect taxes owed to the federal government.

The Church Audit Procedure Act (IRC 7611) provides detailed limitations and procedures for audits of churches initiated by the Internal Revenue Service.

Church Tax Inquiries can only be conducted if an Internal Revenue Service commissioner or high-level treasury official believes on the basis of written evidence that the church is not exempt and sends the church a written inquiry notice disclosing the specific reasons why the inquiry is being conducted. A church tax inquiry is conducted to determine whether an organization is entitled to tax -exempt status or not. A notice must be sent to the church at least fifteen days prior to the examination of the church.

Listed below are some limitations to a church audit.

1. Church records may be examined to determine the amount, if an y, of taxes due,
2. Religious activities may be examined to determine if the organization is a church,
3. Church tax inquiries and examinations must be completed no later than two years after the first notice has been sent,
4. An inquiry, not followed by examination, must be completed within ninety days after the inquiry notice,
5. Only the Internal Revenue Service regional legal counsel can make a determination if a church is not exempt from taxes. The decision to revoke the exemption and/or the assessment of tax must be made in writing,
6. Tax examinations can only be conducted for the three most recent years for business related activities and for six years for non-business activities,
7. If an inquiry or examination does not result in revocation of exempt status, no other church tax inquiry or church tax examination can be conducted within five years from the examination notice date.

Listed below are a few areas the Internal Revenue Service may check during an audit.

1. Financial records and bank statements,
2. Administrative files,
3. Personnel files,

4. The governing documents (Articles of Incorporation, by-laws, Minutes, etc.),
5. Contracts,
6. Audit of all **responsible parties'** individual income tax returns for the same years in question as the church.

Responsible parties include but are not limited to the pastor(s), associate pastor(s), treasurer, secretaries, trustees and/or anyone with knowledge of or control of the church's finances.

RECORD KEEPING

Income received by the church and the Expenses paid out by the church should be monitored and recorded. Utilizing a system that monitors the church's income and expenses is the first good step in developing an effective record keeping system. *As a minister or church official, it is your responsibility to maintain adequate records reflecting the day-to-day activities of the church.*

All records relating to the church's activities such as receipts, cancelled checks, and other records that reflect income and expense information should be kept, at least, until the statute of limitation for that return expires. This is typically three years; however, I would keep them indefinitely. If the church has employees, employment records must be kept for at least four years after the tax is due or paid whichever is later. Again, I recommend keeping your records indefinitely. It is always better to be safe than sorry. Records should be kept for at least four years, and available for IRS review. These records should include, but are not limited to:

1. Your employer identification number.
2. Amounts and dates of all wage, annuity, and pension payments.
3. Names, addresses, social security number, and occupations of employees and recipients.
4. Any employee copies of Form W -2 that were returned to you as undelivered.
5. Dates of employment.
6. Periods for which employees and recipients were paid while absent due to sickness or injury and the amount and weekly rate of payments you or third-party payers made to them.
7. Copies of employees' and recipients' Income tax withholding allowance certificates (Form W-4, W-4P, W4S, and W-4V).
8. Dates and amounts of tax deposits you made and acknowledgement numbers for deposits make by EFTPS.
9. Copies of returns filed, including "nine-forty-one" TeleFile Tax Records and confirmation numbers.

RETIREMENT PLANS

There are many "tax-favored" plans that ministers and lay employees can take advantage of. The term "tax-favored" means that the contributions to the plans on be-half of the employee ordinarily are partially or fully deductible as a pre-tax deduction prior to any income tax being withheld which lowers the income tax liability for the current year. The amount of the contributions from the plan as well as the interest accrued for the plan are not taxable until they are distributed which is usually after retirement when the individual is in a lower income tax bracket.

As with some other governmental requirements, "church plans" are exempt from many of the legal requirements that apply to retirement plans. For example, a "church plan" is exempt from the non-discrimination rules that apply to tax sheltered or "403(b) annuities. "Church plans" also are not required to file an annual Form 5500. A "church plan" is defined by section 414(e) of the Internal Revenue Code and it basically states that a "church plan" includes a plan "maintained for its employees by a church." The income tax regulations, for clarification purposes, defines the term church to include "a religious organization if such organization is an integral part of a church, and is engaged in carrying out the functions of a church, whether as a civil law corporation or otherwise." *Treas. Reg.* 1.414(*e*)-1 *(e).* Listed below are a few of the retirement plans that are available:

1. Individual Retirement Accounts
2. Simplified Employee Pensions
3. Keogh Plans
4. Deferred Compensation Plans
5. Tax Sheltered Annuities
6. Church Retirement Income Accounts
7. Qualified Pension Plans
8. 401k Plans (established prior to June 2, 1986 or after 1996)

When hiring independent contractors, in order to avoid complications the contract should incorporate the following 10 pieces of information clearly, and be recorded in writing between the employer and contractor.

1.) The worker is an independent contractor not an employee.

2.) The worker is restricted from holding out as an employee.

3.) The contractor has the right to control the project.

4.) Terms for either party terminating the arrangement are outlined, including consequences of termination.

5.) The contractor is exempt from all employee benefits.

6.) The contractor is responsible for accounting of all taxes.

7.) If the arrangement is for ongoing services, a specific term subject to renewal is provided.

8.) When possible, the contractor pays all out-of-pocket expenses for work on a project.

9.) When possible, payment is provided on a per-project basis.

10.) Where feasible, contractor will provide tools and equipment necessary to complete the job.

Sample Independent Contractor's Agreement

Independent Contractor's Agreement

[This Independent Contractor's Agreement is provided for informational purposes only. The user should consult with legal counsel before using this document.]

This Independent Contractor's Agreement ("Agreement") is made this ____ day of __________, 199_, by and between __________________________, a __________ corporation ("Corporation"), and ________________________, an independent contractor ("Contractor"), in consideration of the mutual promises made herein, as follows:

Article 1.
Term Of Agreement

This Agreement will become effective on __________, 1991, and will continue in effect *until the services provided for herein have been performed.

*until terminated as provided herein.

*for a period of __________ years unless sooner terminated.

Article 2.
Services to be Performed by Contractor

2.1. Specific Services. Contractor agrees to [DESCRIBE IN DETAIL THE SERVICES TO BE PERFORMED] OR

Contractor agrees to perform the services specified in the "Description of Services" attached to this Agreement as Exhibit A and incorporated herein by this reference.

2.2. Method of Performing Services. Contractor will determine the method, details, and means of performing the above-described services.

2.3. Employment of Assistants. Contractor may, at Contractor's own expense, employ such assistants as Contractor deems necessary to perform the services required of Contractor by this Agreement. Corporation may not control, direct, or supervise Contractor's assistants or employees in the performance of those services.

Article 3.
Compensation

3.1. Flat Rate. In consideration for the services to be performed by Contractor, Corporation agrees to pay Contractor the sum of ____________________________ Dollars ($__________).

OR

Hourly or Per Diem Compensation with Maximum and Minimum Stated. In consideration for the services to be performed by Contractor, Corporation agrees to pay to Contractor the sum of ______________ Dollars ($____) per *hour/day/month. In no event, however, will the compensation paid to Contractor be less than ____________________________ Dollars ($_____) per *hour/day/month, or more than Dollars ($_____) per *hour/day/month.

OR

Retainer. Corporation agrees to pay Contractor for the services set forth in Article 2 above, the sum of ________ ____________________ ($__________) as a retainer at the time of execution of this Agreement. In addition to the retainer, Corporation agrees to pay monthly any and all reasonable and necessary expenses incurred by Contractor on behalf of Corporation in connection with the services described in Article 2 of this Agreement.

3.2. Date for Payment of Compensation. For services rendered under this Agreement,

4.4. Workers' Compensation. Contractor agrees to provide workers' compensation insurance for Contractor's employees and agents and agrees to hold harmless and indemnify Corporation for any and all claims arising out of any injury, disability, or death of any of Contractor's employees or agents.

4.5. Liability Insurance. Contractor agrees to maintain a policy of insurance in the minimum amount of ________________ Dollars ($__________) to cover any negligent acts committed by Contractor or Contractor's employees or agents during the performance of any duties under this Agreement. Contractor further agrees to hold Corporation free and harmless from any and all claims arising from any such negligent act or omission.

OR

Limited Liability. Contractor will not be liable to Corporation, or to anyone who may claim any right due to a relationship with Corporation, for any acts or omissions in the performance of services under the terms of this Agreement or on the part of employees or agents of Contractor unless such acts or omissions are due to willful misconduct. Corporation will indemnify and hold Contractor free and harmless from any obligations, costs, claims, judgments, attorneys' fees, and attachments arising from, growing out of, or in any way connected with the services rendered to Corporation under the terms of this Agreement, unless Contractor is judged by a court of competent jurisdiction to be guilty of willful misconduct.

4.6. Assignment. Neither this Agreement nor any duties or obligations under this Agreement may be assigned by Contractor without the prior written consent of Corporation.

Article 5.
Obligations of Corporation

5.1. Cooperation of Corporation. Corporation agrees to comply with all reasonable requests of Contractor [and to provide access to all documents reasonably] necessary to the performance of Contractor's duties under this Agreement.

5.2. Place of Work. Corporation agrees to furnish space on Corporation's premises for use by Contractor while performing the above-described services.

5.3. Assignment. Neither this Agreement nor any duties or obligations under this Agreement may be assigned by Corporation without the prior written consent of Contractor.

Article 6.
Termination Of Agreement

6.1. Expiration of Agreement. Unless otherwise terminated as provided herein, this Agreement shall continue in force for a period of ________________ months/years OR [until the services provided for herein have been fully and completely performed] and shall thereupon terminate unless renewed in writing by both parties.

OR

Termination Upon Notice. Notwithstanding any other provisions of this Agreement, either party hereto may terminate this Agreement at any time by giving ____________________________ written notice to the other party. Unless otherwise terminated as provided herein, this Agreement shall continue in force

*for a period of ___________ months/years.

*until the services provided for herein have been fully and completely performed.

6.2. Termination on Occurrence of Stated Events. This Agreement shall terminate automatically on the occurrence of (1) bankruptcy or insolvency of either party; (2) sale of the business of either party; (3) death of the Contractor; or (4) assignment of this Agreement by either party without the express written consent of the other party.

6.3. Termination by Corporation for Default of Contractor. Should Contractor default in the performance of this Agreement or materially breach any of its provisions, Corporation, at Corporation's option, may terminate this Agreement by giving written notification to Contractor. For the purposes of this paragraph, material breach of this Agreement shall include, but not be limited to,

____.

6.4. Termination by Contractor for Default of Corporation. Should Corporation default in the performance of this Agreement or materially breach any of its provisions, Contractor, at Contractor's option, may terminate this Agreement by giving written notification to Corporation. For the purposes of this paragraph, material breach of this Agreement shall include, but not be limited to,

____.

6.5. Termination for Failure to Make Agreed-Upon Payments. Should Corporation fail to pay Contractor all or any part of the compensation set forth in Paragraphs 3.1 and 3.2 of this Agreement on the due date, Contractor, at Contractor's option, may terminate this Agreement if the failure is not remedied by Corporation within thirty (30) days from the date payment is due.

Article 7.
General Provisions

7.1. Notices. Any notices to be given hereunder by either party to the other may be effected either by personal delivery or by mail, registered or certified, postage prepaid with return receipt requested. Mailed notices shall be addressed to the parties at the addresses appearing in the introductory paragraph of this Agreement, but each party may change that address by written notice in accordance with this paragraph. Notices delivered personally shall be deemed communicated as of the date of actual receipt; mailed notices shall be deemed communicated as of three (3) days after the date of mailing.

7.2. Entire Agreement. This Agreement supersedes any and all agreements, either oral or in writing, between the parties hereto with respect to the rendering of services by Contractor for Corporation, and contains all of the covenants and agreements between the parties with respect to the rendering of such services in any manner whatsoever. Each party to this Agreement acknowledges that no representations, inducements, promises, or agreements, orally or otherwise, have been made by any party, or anyone acting on behalf of any party, which are not embodied herein, and that no other agreement, statement, or promise not contained in this Agreement shall be valid or binding. Any modification of this Agreement will be effective only if it is in writing signed by the party to be charged.

7.3. Partial Invalidity. If any provision of this Agreement is held by a court of competent jurisdiction to be invalid, void, or unenforceable, the remaining provisions shall nevertheless continue in full force without being impaired or invalidated in any way.

7.4. Payment of Moneys Due Deceased Contractor. If Contractor dies prior to the completion of this Agreement, any moneys that may be due Contractor from Corporation under this Agreement as of the date of death shall be paid to Contractor's executors, administrators, heirs, personal representatives, successors, and assigns.

[OPTIONAL]

7.5. Arbitration. Any controversy between the parties hereto involving the construction or application of any of the terms, covenants, or conditions of this Agreement will, on the written request of one party served on the other, be submitted to arbitration. The arbitration will comply with and be governed by the provisions of the California Arbitration Act, Sections 1280 through 1294.2 of the California Code of Civil Procedure.

The parties will each appoint one person to hear and determine the dispute and if they are unable to agree, then the two persons so chosen will select a third impartial arbitrator whose decision will be final and conclusive on both parties. The cost of arbitration will be borne in such proportions as the arbitrators decide.

OR

Any controversy or claim arising out of or relating to this Agreement or the breach thereof will be settled by arbitration in accordance with the rules of the American Arbitration Association, and judgment upon the award rendered by the arbitrator(s) may be entered in any court having jurisdiction thereof.

[OPTIONAL]

7.6. Liquidated Damages. It is agreed that in the event of a breach of this Agreement by Contractor, it would be impracticable or extremely difficult to fix the actual damages and, therefore, Contractor will pay to Corporation as liquidated damages and not as a penalty, the sum of ________________________ Dollars ($__________), which represents a reasonable compensation for the loss incurred because of the breach.

7.7. Attorneys' Fees. If any action at law or in equity, including an action for declaratory relief, is brought to enforce or interpret the terms of this Agreement, the prevailing party shall be entitled to reasonable attorneys' fees, which may be set by the court in the same action or in a separate action brought for that purpose, in addition to any other relief to which that party may be entitled.

7.8. Governing Law. This Agreement shall be governed by and construed in accordance with the laws of the State of California.

Executed at ______________________, California, on the date and year first written above.

"Corporation" ___________________________________, a ______________ corporation

By: _________________________________

"Contractor" _____________________________________*

a2/drs/10/100/061
Revised: 6/10/93

Sample IRS Blank Forms

- Form 1023 – Application for Recognition of Exemption Under Section 501(c)(3) of the Internal Revenue Code
- Form 1040
- Form 1040 Schedule A
- Form 1040 Self-Employment
- Form SS8
- Form W-3
- Form 941
- Form 1040ES
- Form 1040 Schedule C
- Form 1099
- Form W-2
- Form W-4
- Form 2106
- Form 4361
- Form 4029

Form **1023** (Rev. June 2006) Department of the Treasury Internal Revenue Service

Application for Recognition of Exemption Under Section 501(c)(3) of the Internal Revenue Code

OMB No. 1545-0056

Note: *If exempt status is approved, this application will be open for public inspection.*

Use the instructions to complete this application and for a definition of all ***bold*** *items.* For additional help, call IRS Exempt Organizations Customer Account Services toll-free at 1-877-829-5500. Visit our website at **www.irs.gov** for forms and publications. If the required information and documents are not submitted with payment of the appropriate user fee, the application may be returned to you.

Attach additional sheets to this application if you need more space to answer fully. Put your name and EIN on each sheet and identify each answer by Part and line number. Complete Parts I - XI of Form 1023 and submit only those Schedules (A through H) that apply to you.

Part I Identification of Applicant

1 Full name of organization (exactly as it appears in your **organizing document**)		2 c/o Name (if applicable)
3 Mailing address (Number and street) (see instructions)	Room/Suite	4 Employer Identification Number (EIN)
City or town, state or country, and ZIP + 4		5 Month the annual accounting period ends (01 – 12)
6 Primary contact (officer, director, trustee, or **authorized representative**) a Name:		b Phone:
		c Fax: (optional)

7 Are you represented by an authorized representative, such as an attorney or accountant? If "Yes," provide the authorized representative's name, and the name and address of the authorized representative's firm. Include a completed Form 2848, *Power of Attorney and Declaration of Representative*, with your application if you would like us to communicate with your representative. ☐ Yes ☐ No

8 Was a person who is not one of your officers, directors, trustees, employees, or an authorized representative listed in line 7, paid, or promised payment, to help plan, manage, or advise you about the structure or activities of your organization, or about your financial or tax matters? If "Yes," provide the person's name, the name and address of the person's firm, the amounts paid or promised to be paid, and describe that person's role. ☐ Yes ☐ No

9a Organization's website:

b Organization's email: (optional)

10 Certain organizations are not required to file an information return (Form 990 or Form 990-EZ). If you are granted tax-exemption, are you claiming to be excused from filing Form 990 or Form 990-EZ? If "Yes," explain. See the instructions for a description of organizations not required to file Form 990 or Form 990-EZ. ☐ Yes ☐ No

11 Date incorporated if a corporation, or formed, if other than a corporation. (MM/DD/YYYY) / /

12 Were you formed under the laws of a foreign country? If "Yes," state the country. ☐ Yes ☐ No

Part II Organizational Structure

You must be a corporation (including a limited liability company), an unincorporated association, or a trust to be tax exempt. (See instructions.) **DO NOT file this form unless you can check "Yes" on lines 1, 2, 3, or 4.**

1 Are you a **corporation**? If "Yes," attach a copy of your articles of incorporation showing certification of filing with the appropriate state agency. Include copies of any amendments to your articles and be sure they also show state filing certification. ☐ Yes ☐ No

2 Are you a **limited liability company (LLC)**? If "Yes," attach a copy of your articles of organization showing certification of filing with the appropriate state agency. Also, if you adopted an operating agreement, attach a copy. Include copies of any amendments to your articles and be sure they show state filing certification. Refer to the instructions for circumstances when an LLC should not file its own exemption application. ☐ Yes ☐ No

3 Are you an **unincorporated association**? If "Yes," attach a copy of your articles of association, constitution, or other similar organizing document that is dated and includes at least two signatures. Include signed and dated copies of any amendments. ☐ Yes ☐ No

4a Are you a **trust**? If "Yes," attach a signed and dated copy of your trust agreement. Include signed and dated copies of any amendments. ☐ Yes ☐ No

b Have you been funded? If "No," explain how you are formed without anything of value placed in trust. ☐ Yes ☐ No

5 Have you adopted bylaws? If "Yes," attach a current copy showing date of adoption. If "No," explain how your officers, directors, or trustees are selected. ☐ Yes ☐ No

Part III Required Provisions in Your Organizing Document

The following questions are designed to ensure that when you file this application, your organizing document contains the required provisions to meet the organizational test under section 501(c)(3). Unless you can check the boxes in both lines 1 and 2, your organizing document does not meet the organizational test. **DO NOT file this application until you have amended your organizing document.** Submit your original and amended organizing documents (showing state filing certification if you are a corporation or an LLC) with your application.

1 Section 501(c)(3) requires that your organizing document state your exempt purpose(s), such as charitable, religious, educational, and/or scientific purposes. Check the box to confirm that your organizing document meets this requirement. Describe specifically where your organizing document meets this requirement, such as a reference to a particular article or section in your organizing document. Refer to the instructions for exempt purpose language. Location of Purpose Clause (Page, Article, and Paragraph): ______________ ☐

2a Section 501(c)(3) requires that upon dissolution of your organization, your remaining assets must be used exclusively for exempt purposes, such as charitable, religious, educational, and/or scientific purposes. Check the box on line 2a to confirm that your organizing document meets this requirement by express provision for the distribution of assets upon dissolution. If you rely on state law for your dissolution provision, do not check the box on line 2a and go to line 2c. ☐

2b If you checked the box on line 2a, specify the location of your dissolution clause (Page, Article, and Paragraph). Do not complete line 2c if you checked box 2a. ______________

2c See the instructions for information about the operation of state law in your particular state. Check this box if you rely on operation of state law for your dissolution provision and indicate the state: ______________ ☐

Part IV Narrative Description of Your Activities

Using an attachment, describe your *past, present,* and *planned* activities in a narrative. If you believe that you have already provided some of this information in response to other parts of this application, you may summarize that information here and refer to the specific parts of the application for supporting details. You may also attach representative copies of newsletters, brochures, or similar documents for supporting details to this narrative. Remember that if this application is approved, it will be open for public inspection. Therefore, your narrative description of activities should be thorough and accurate. Refer to the instructions for information that must be included in your description.

Part V Compensation and Other Financial Arrangements With Your Officers, Directors, Trustees, Employees, and Independent Contractors

1a List the names, titles, and mailing addresses of all of your officers, directors, and trustees. For each person listed, state their total annual **compensation**, or proposed compensation, for all services to the organization, whether as an officer, employee, or other position. Use actual figures, if available. Enter "none" if no compensation is or will be paid. If additional space is needed, attach a separate sheet. Refer to the instructions for information on what to include as compensation.

Name	Title	Mailing address	Compensation amount (annual actual or estimated)

Part V **Compensation and Other Financial Arrangements With Your Officers, Directors, Trustees, Employees, and Independent Contractors** *(Continued)*

b List the names, titles, and mailing addresses of each of your five highest compensated employees who receive or will receive compensation of more than $50,000 per year. Use the actual figure, if available. Refer to the instructions for information on what to include as compensation. Do not include officers, directors, or trustees listed in line 1a.

Name	Title	Mailing address	Compensation amount (annual actual or estimated)

c List the names, names of businesses, and mailing addresses of your five highest compensated independent contractors that receive or will receive compensation of more than $50,000 per year. Use the actual figure, if available. Refer to the instructions for information on what to include as compensation.

Name	Title	Mailing address	Compensation amount (annual actual or estimated)

The following "Yes" or "No" questions relate to *past, present, or planned* relationships, transactions, or agreements with your officers, directors, trustees, highest compensated employees, and highest compensated independent contractors listed in lines 1a, 1b, and 1c.

2a Are any of your officers, directors, or trustees related to each other through family or business relationships? If "Yes," identify the individuals and explain the relationship. ☐ Yes ☐ No

b Do you have a business relationship with any of your officers, directors, or trustees other than through their position as an officer, director, or trustee? If "Yes," identify the individuals and describe the business relationship with each of your officers, directors, or trustees. ☐ Yes ☐ No

c Are any of your officers, directors, or trustees related to your highest compensated employees or highest compensated independent contractors listed on lines 1b or 1c through family or business relationships? If "Yes," identify the individuals and explain the relationship. ☐ Yes ☐ No

3a For each of your officers, directors, trustees, highest compensated employees, and highest compensated independent contractors listed on lines 1a, 1b, or 1c, attach a list showing their name, qualifications, average hours worked, and duties.

b Do any of your officers, directors, trustees, highest compensated employees, and highest compensated independent contractors listed on lines 1a, 1b, or 1c receive compensation from any other organizations, whether tax exempt or taxable, that are related to you through common control? If "Yes," identify the individuals, explain the relationship between you and the other organization, and describe the compensation arrangement. ☐ Yes ☐ No

4 In establishing the compensation for your officers, directors, trustees, highest compensated employees, and highest compensated independent contractors listed on lines 1a, 1b, and 1c, the following practices are recommended, although they are not required to obtain exemption. Answer "Yes" to all the practices you use.

a Do you or will the individuals that approve compensation arrangements follow a conflict of interest policy? ☐ Yes ☐ No
b Do you or will you approve compensation arrangements in advance of paying compensation? ☐ Yes ☐ No
c Do you or will you document in writing the date and terms of approved compensation arrangements? ☐ Yes ☐ No

Part V **Compensation and Other Financial Arrangements With Your Officers, Directors, Trustees, Employees, and Independent Contractors** *(Continued)*

d Do you or will you record in writing the decision made by each individual who decided or voted on compensation arrangements? ☐ Yes ☐ No

e Do you or will you approve compensation arrangements based on information about compensation paid by similarly situated taxable or tax-exempt organizations for similar services, current compensation surveys compiled by independent firms, or actual written offers from similarly situated organizations? Refer to the instructions for Part V, lines 1a, 1b, and 1c, for information on what to include as compensation. ☐ Yes ☐ No

f Do you or will you record in writing both the information on which you relied to base your decision and its source? ☐ Yes ☐ No

g If you answered "No" to any item on lines 4a through 4f, describe how you set compensation that is reasonable for your officers, directors, trustees, highest compensated employees, and highest compensated independent contractors listed in Part V, lines 1a, 1b, and 1c.

5a Have you adopted a conflict of interest policy consistent with the sample conflict of interest policy in Appendix A to the instructions? If "Yes," provide a copy of the policy and explain how the policy has been adopted, such as by resolution of your governing board. If "No," answer lines 5b and 5c. ☐ Yes ☐ No

b What procedures will you follow to assure that persons who have a conflict of interest will not have influence over you for setting their own compensation?

c What procedures will you follow to assure that persons who have a conflict of interest will not have influence over you regarding business deals with themselves?

Note: A conflict of interest policy is recommended though it is not required to obtain exemption. Hospitals, see Schedule C, Section I, line 14.

6a Do you or will you compensate any of your officers, directors, trustees, highest compensated employees, and highest compensated independent contractors listed in lines 1a, 1b, or 1c through non-fixed payments, such as discretionary bonuses or revenue-based payments? If "Yes," describe all non-fixed compensation arrangements, including how the amounts are determined, who is eligible for such arrangements, whether you place a limitation on total compensation, and how you determine or will determine that you pay no more than reasonable compensation for services. Refer to the instructions for Part V, lines 1a, 1b, and 1c, for information on what to include as compensation. ☐ Yes ☐ No

b Do you or will you compensate any of your employees, other than your officers, directors, trustees, or your five highest compensated employees who receive or will receive compensation of more than $50,000 per year, through non-fixed payments, such as discretionary bonuses or revenue-based payments? If "Yes," describe all non-fixed compensation arrangements, including how the amounts are or will be determined, who is or will be eligible for such arrangements, whether you place or will place a limitation on total compensation, and how you determine or will determine that you pay no more than reasonable compensation for services. Refer to the instructions for Part V, lines 1a, 1b, and 1c, for information on what to include as compensation. ☐ Yes ☐ No

7a Do you or will you purchase any goods, services, or assets from any of your officers, directors, trustees, highest compensated employees, or highest compensated independent contractors listed in lines 1a, 1b, or 1c? If "Yes," describe any such purchase that you made or intend to make, from whom you make or will make such purchases, how the terms are or will be negotiated at arm's length, and explain how you determine or will determine that you pay no more than fair market value. Attach copies of any written contracts or other agreements relating to such purchases. ☐ Yes ☐ No

b Do you or will you sell any goods, services, or assets to any of your officers, directors, trustees, highest compensated employees, or highest compensated independent contractors listed in lines 1a, 1b, or 1c? If "Yes," describe any such sales that you made or intend to make, to whom you make or will make such sales, how the terms are or will be negotiated at arm's length, and explain how you determine or will determine you are or will be paid at least fair market value. Attach copies of any written contracts or other agreements relating to such sales. ☐ Yes ☐ No

8a Do you or will you have any leases, contracts, loans, or other agreements with your officers, directors, trustees, highest compensated employees, or highest compensated independent contractors listed in lines 1a, 1b, or 1c? If "Yes," provide the information requested in lines 8b through 8f. ☐ Yes ☐ No

b Describe any written or oral arrangements that you made or intend to make.

c Identify with whom you have or will have such arrangements.

d Explain how the terms are or will be negotiated at arm's length.

e Explain how you determine you pay no more than fair market value or you are paid at least fair market value.

f Attach copies of any signed leases, contracts, loans, or other agreements relating to such arrangements.

9a Do you or will you have any leases, contracts, loans, or other agreements with any organization in which any of your officers, directors, or trustees are also officers, directors, or trustees, or in which any individual officer, director, or trustee owns more than a 35% interest? If "Yes," provide the information requested in lines 9b through 9f. ☐ Yes ☐ No

Part V **Compensation and Other Financial Arrangements With Your Officers, Directors, Trustees, Employees, and Independent Contractors** *(Continued)*

b Describe any written or oral arrangements you made or intend to make.

c Identify with whom you have or will have such arrangements.

d Explain how the terms are or will be negotiated at arm's length.

e Explain how you determine or will determine you pay no more than fair market value or that you are paid at least fair market value.

f Attach a copy of any signed leases, contracts, loans, or other agreements relating to such arrangements.

Part VI **Your Members and Other Individuals and Organizations That Receive Benefits From You**

The following "Yes" or "No" questions relate to goods, services, and funds you provide to individuals and organizations as part of your activities. Your answers should pertain to *past, present,* and *planned* activities. (See instructions.)

1a In carrying out your exempt purposes, do you provide goods, services, or funds to individuals? If "Yes," describe each program that provides goods, services, or funds to individuals. ☐ Yes ☐ No

b In carrying out your exempt purposes, do you provide goods, services, or funds to organizations? If "Yes," describe each program that provides goods, services, or funds to organizations. ☐ Yes ☐ No

2 Do any of your programs limit the provision of goods, services, or funds to a specific individual or group of specific individuals? For example, answer "Yes," if goods, services, or funds are provided only for a particular individual, your members, individuals who work for a particular employer, or graduates of a particular school. If "Yes," explain the limitation and how recipients are selected for each program. ☐ Yes ☐ No

3 Do any individuals who receive goods, services, or funds through your programs have a family or business relationship with any officer, director, trustee, or with any of your highest compensated employees or highest compensated independent contractors listed in Part V, lines 1a, 1b, and 1c? If "Yes," explain how these related individuals are eligible for goods, services, or funds. ☐ Yes ☐ No

Part VII **Your History**

The following "Yes" or "No" questions relate to your history. (See instructions.)

1 Are you a successor to another organization? Answer "Yes," if you have taken or will take over the activities of another organization; you took over 25% or more of the fair market value of the net assets of another organization; or you were established upon the conversion of an organization from for-profit to non-profit status. If "Yes," complete Schedule G. ☐ Yes ☐ No

2 Are you submitting this application more than 27 months after the end of the month in which you were legally formed? If "Yes," complete Schedule E. ☐ Yes ☐ No

Part VIII **Your Specific Activities**

The following "Yes" or "No" questions relate to specific activities that you may conduct. Check the appropriate box. Your answers should pertain to *past, present,* and *planned* activities. (See instructions.)

1 Do you support or oppose candidates in political campaigns in any way? If "Yes," explain. ☐ Yes ☐ No

2a Do you attempt to influence legislation? If "Yes," explain how you attempt to influence legislation and complete line 2b. If "No," go to line 3a. ☐ Yes ☐ No

b Have you made or are you making an election to have your legislative activities measured by expenditures by filing Form 5768? If "Yes," attach a copy of the Form 5768 that was already filed or attach a completed Form 5768 that you are filing with this application. If "No," describe whether your attempts to influence legislation are a substantial part of your activities. Include the time and money spent on your attempts to influence legislation as compared to your total activities. ☐ Yes ☐ No

3a Do you or will you operate bingo or gaming activities? If "Yes," describe who conducts them, and list all revenue received or expected to be received and expenses paid or expected to be paid in operating these activities. Revenue and expenses should be provided for the time periods specified in Part IX, Financial Data. ☐ Yes ☐ No

b Do you or will you enter into contracts or other agreements with individuals or organizations to conduct bingo or gaming for you? If "Yes," describe any written or oral arrangements that you made or intend to make, identify with whom you have or will have such arrangements, explain how the terms are or will be negotiated at arm's length, and explain how you determine or will determine you pay no more than fair market value or you will be paid at least fair market value. Attach copies or any written contracts or other agreements relating to such arrangements. ☐ Yes ☐ No

c List the states and local jurisdictions, including Indian Reservations, in which you conduct or will conduct gaming or bingo.

Part VIII Your Specific Activities (Continued)

4a Do you or will you undertake fundraising? If "Yes," check all the fundraising programs you do or will conduct. (See instructions.) ☐ Yes ☐ No

- ☐ mail solicitations
- ☐ email solicitations
- ☐ personal solicitations
- ☐ vehicle, boat, plane, or similar donations
- ☐ foundation grant solicitations
- ☐ phone solicitations
- ☐ accept donations on your website
- ☐ receive donations from another organization's website
- ☐ government grant solicitations
- ☐ Other

Attach a description of each fundraising program.

b Do you or will you have written or oral contracts with any individuals or organizations to raise funds for you? If "Yes," describe these activities. Include all revenue and expenses from these activities and state who conducts them. Revenue and expenses should be provided for the time periods specified in Part IX, Financial Data. Also, attach a copy of any contracts or agreements. ☐ Yes ☐ No

c Do you or will you engage in fundraising activities for other organizations? If "Yes," describe these arrangements. Include a description of the organizations for which you raise funds and attach copies of all contracts or agreements. ☐ Yes ☐ No

d List all states and local jurisdictions in which you conduct fundraising. For each state or local jurisdiction listed, specify whether you fundraise for your own organization, you fundraise for another organization, or another organization fundraises for you.

e Do you or will you maintain separate accounts for any contributor under which the contributor has the right to advise on the use or distribution of funds? Answer "Yes" if the donor may provide advice on the types of investments, distributions from the types of investments, or the distribution from the donor's contribution account. If "Yes," describe this program, including the type of advice that may be provided and submit copies of any written materials provided to donors. ☐ Yes ☐ No

5 Are you affiliated with a governmental unit? If "Yes," explain. ☐ Yes ☐ No

6a Do you or will you engage in economic development? If "Yes," describe your program. ☐ Yes ☐ No

b Describe in full who benefits from your economic development activities and how the activities promote exempt purposes.

7a Do or will persons other than your employees or volunteers develop your facilities? If "Yes," describe each facility, the role of the developer, and any business or family relationship(s) between the developer and your officers, directors, or trustees. ☐ Yes ☐ No

b Do or will persons other than your employees or volunteers manage your activities or facilities? If "Yes," describe each activity and facility, the role of the manager, and any business or family relationship(s) between the manager and your officers, directors, or trustees. ☐ Yes ☐ No

c If there is a business or family relationship between any manager or developer and your officers, directors, or trustees, identify the individuals, explain the relationship, describe how contracts are negotiated at arm's length so that you pay no more than fair market value, and submit a copy of any contracts or other agreements.

8 Do you or will you enter into joint ventures, including partnerships or limited liability companies treated as partnerships, in which you share profits and losses with partners other than section 501(c)(3) organizations? If "Yes," describe the activities of these joint ventures in which you participate. ☐ Yes ☐ No

9a Are you applying for exemption as a childcare organization under section 501(k)? If "Yes," answer lines 9b through 9d. If "No," go to line 10. ☐ Yes ☐ No

b Do you provide child care so that parents or caretakers of children you care for can be gainfully employed (see instructions)? If "No," explain how you qualify as a childcare organization described in section 501(k). ☐ Yes ☐ No

c Of the children for whom you provide child care, are 85% or more of them cared for by you to enable their parents or caretakers to be gainfully employed (see instructions)? If "No," explain how you qualify as a childcare organization described in section 501(k). ☐ Yes ☐ No

d Are your services available to the general public? If "No," describe the specific group of people for whom your activities are available. Also, see the instructions and explain how you qualify as a childcare organization described in section 501(k). ☐ Yes ☐ No

10 Do you or will you publish, own, or have rights in music, literature, tapes, artworks, choreography, scientific discoveries, or other intellectual property? If "Yes," explain. Describe who owns or will own any copyrights, patents, or trademarks, whether fees are or will be charged, how the fees are determined, and how any items are or will be produced, distributed, and marketed. ☐ Yes ☐ No

Part VIII Your Specific Activities *(Continued)*

11 Do you or will you accept contributions of: real property; conservation easements; closely held securities; intellectual property such as patents, trademarks, and copyrights; works of music or art; licenses; royalties; automobiles, boats, planes, or other vehicles; or collectibles of any type? If "Yes," describe each type of contribution, any conditions imposed by the donor on the contribution, and any agreements with the donor regarding the contribution. ☐ Yes ☐ No

12a Do you or will you operate in a **foreign country** or countries? If "Yes," answer lines 12b through 12d. If "No," go to line 13a. ☐ Yes ☐ No

b Name the foreign countries and regions within the countries in which you operate.

c Describe your operations in each country and region in which you operate.

d Describe how your operations in each country and region further your exempt purposes.

13a Do you or will you make grants, loans, or other distributions to organization(s)? If "Yes," answer lines 13b through 13g. If "No," go to line 14a. ☐ Yes ☐ No

b Describe how your grants, loans, or other distributions to organizations further your exempt purposes.

c Do you have written contracts with each of these organizations? If "Yes," attach a copy of each contract. ☐ Yes ☐ No

d Identify each recipient organization and any **relationship** between you and the recipient organization.

e Describe the records you keep with respect to the grants, loans, or other distributions you make.

f Describe your selection process, including whether you do any of the following:

(i) Do you require an application form? If "Yes," attach a copy of the form. ☐ Yes ☐ No

(ii) Do you require a grant proposal? If "Yes," describe whether the grant proposal specifies your responsibilities and those of the grantee, obligates the grantee to use the grant funds only for the purposes for which the grant was made, provides for periodic written reports concerning the use of grant funds, requires a final written report and an accounting of how grant funds were used, and acknowledges your authority to withhold and/or recover grant funds in case such funds are, or appear to be, misused. ☐ Yes ☐ No

g Describe your procedures for oversight of distributions that assure you the resources are used to further your exempt purposes, including whether you require periodic and final reports on the use of resources.

14a Do you or will you make grants, loans, or other distributions to foreign organizations? If "Yes," answer lines 14b through 14f. If "No," go to line 15. ☐ Yes ☐ No

b Provide the name of each foreign organization, the country and regions within a country in which each foreign organization operates, and describe any relationship you have with each foreign organization.

c Does any foreign organization listed in line 14b accept contributions earmarked for a specific country or specific organization? If "Yes," list all earmarked organizations or countries. ☐ Yes ☐ No

d Do your contributors know that you have ultimate authority to use contributions made to you at your discretion for purposes consistent with your exempt purposes? If "Yes," describe how you relay this information to contributors. ☐ Yes ☐ No

e Do you or will you make pre-grant inquiries about the recipient organization? If "Yes," describe these inquiries, including whether you inquire about the recipient's financial status, its tax-exempt status under the Internal Revenue Code, its ability to accomplish the purpose for which the resources are provided, and other relevant information. ☐ Yes ☐ No

f Do you or will you use any additional procedures to ensure that your distributions to foreign organizations are used in furtherance of your exempt purposes? If "Yes," describe these procedures, including site visits by your employees or compliance checks by impartial experts, to verify that grant funds are being used appropriately. ☐ Yes ☐ No

Part VIII Your Specific Activities (Continued)

15	Do you have a close connection with any organizations? If "Yes," explain.	☐ Yes	☐ No
16	Are you applying for exemption as a cooperative hospital service organization under section 501(e)? If "Yes," explain.	☐ Yes	☐ No
17	Are you applying for exemption as a cooperative service organization of operating educational organizations under section 501(f)? If "Yes," explain.	☐ Yes	☐ No
18	Are you applying for exemption as a charitable risk pool under section 501(n)? If "Yes," explain.	☐ Yes	☐ No
19	Do you or will you operate a school? If "Yes," complete Schedule B. Answer "Yes," whether you operate a school as your main function or as a secondary activity.	☐ Yes	☐ No
20	Is your main function to provide hospital or medical care? If "Yes," complete Schedule C.	☐ Yes	☐ No
21	Do you or will you provide low-income housing or housing for the elderly or handicapped? If "Yes," complete Schedule F.	☐ Yes	☐ No
22	Do you or will you provide scholarships, fellowships, educational loans, or other educational grants to individuals, including grants for travel, study, or other similar purposes? If "Yes," complete Schedule H. Note: Private foundations may use Schedule H to request advance approval of individual grant procedures.	☐ Yes	☐ No

Part IX Financial Data

For purposes of this schedule, years in existence refer to completed tax years. If in existence 4 or more years, complete the schedule for the most recent 4 tax years. If in existence more than 1 year but less than 4 years, complete the statements for each year in existence and provide projections of your likely revenues and expenses based on a reasonable and good faith estimate of your future finances for a total of 3 years of financial information. If in existence less than 1 year, provide projections of your likely revenues and expenses for the current year and the 2 following years, based on a reasonable and good faith estimate of your future finances for a total of 3 years of financial information. (See instructions.)

A. Statement of Revenues and Expenses

	Type of revenue or expense	Current tax year	3 prior tax years or 2 succeeding tax years			
		(a) From .... To	(b) From .... To	(c) From .... To	(d) From .... To	(e) Provide Total for (a) through (d)
Revenues	1 Gifts, grants, and contributions received (do not include unusual grants)					
	2 Membership fees received					
	3 Gross investment income					
	4 Net unrelated business income					
	5 Taxes levied for your benefit					
	6 Value of services or facilities furnished by a governmental unit without charge (not including the value of services generally furnished to the public without charge)					
	7 Any revenue not otherwise listed above or in lines 9–12 below (attach an itemized list)					
	8 Total of lines 1 through 7					
	9 Gross receipts from admissions, merchandise sold or services performed, or furnishing of facilities in any activity that is related to your exempt purposes (attach itemized list)					
	10 Total of lines 8 and 9					
	11 Net gain or loss on sale of capital assets (attach schedule and see instructions)					
	12 Unusual grants					
	13 Total Revenue Add lines 10 through 12					
Expenses	14 Fundraising expenses					
	15 Contributions, gifts, grants, and similar amounts paid out (attach an itemized list)					
	16 Disbursements to or for the benefit of members (attach an itemized list)					
	17 Compensation of officers, directors, and trustees					
	18 Other salaries and wages					
	19 Interest expense					
	20 Occupancy (rent, utilities, etc.)					
	21 Depreciation and depletion					
	22 Professional fees					
	23 Any expense not otherwise classified, such as program services (attach itemized list)					
	24 Total Expenses Add lines 14 through 23					

Part IX Financial Data *(Continued)*

B. Balance Sheet (for your most recently completed tax year)			Year End:
	Assets		(Whole dollars)
1	Cash	1	
2	Accounts receivable, net	2	
3	Inventories	3	
4	Bonds and notes receivable (attach an itemized list)	4	
5	Corporate stocks (attach an itemized list)	5	
6	Loans receivable (attach an itemized list)	6	
7	Other investments (attach an itemized list)	7	
8	Depreciable and depletable assets (attach an itemized list)	8	
9	Land	9	
10	Other assets (attach an itemized list)	10	
11	Total Assets (add lines 1 through 10)	11	
	Liabilities		
12	Accounts payable	12	
13	Contributions, gifts, grants, etc. payable	13	
14	Mortgages and notes payable (attach an itemized list)	14	
15	Other liabilities (attach an itemized list)	15	
16	Total Liabilities (add lines 12 through 15)	16	
	Fund Balances or Net Assets		
17	Total fund balances or net assets	17	
18	Total Liabilities and Fund Balances or Net Assets (add lines 16 and 17)	18	

19 Have there been any substantial changes in your assets or liabilities since the end of the period shown above? If "Yes," explain. ☐ Yes ☐ No

Part X Public Charity Status

Part X is designed to classify you as an organization that is either a **private foundation** or a **public charity**. Public charity status is a more favorable tax status than private foundation status. If you are a private foundation, Part X is designed to further determine whether you are a **private operating foundation**. (See instructions.)

1a Are you a private foundation? If "Yes," go to line 1b. If "No," go to line 5 and proceed as instructed. If you are unsure, see the instructions. ☐ Yes ☐ No

b As a private foundation, section 508(e) requires special provisions in your organizing document in addition to those that apply to all organizations described in section 501(c)(3). Check the box to confirm that your organizing document meets this requirement, whether by express provision or by reliance on operation of state law. Attach a statement that describes specifically where your organizing document meets this requirement, such as a reference to a particular article or section in your organizing document or by operation of state law. See the instructions, including Appendix B, for information about the special provisions that need to be contained in your organizing document. Go to line 2. ☐

2 Are you a private operating foundation? To be a private operating foundation you must engage directly in the active conduct of charitable, religious, educational, and similar activities, as opposed to indirectly carrying out these activities by providing grants to individuals or other organizations. If "Yes," go to line 3. If "No," go to the signature section of Part XI. ☐ Yes ☐ No

3 Have you existed for one or more years? If "Yes," attach financial information showing that you are a private operating foundation; go to the signature section of Part XI. If "No," continue to line 4. ☐ Yes ☐ No

4 Have you attached either (1) an affidavit or opinion of counsel, (including a written affidavit or opinion from a certified public accountant or accounting firm with expertise regarding this tax law matter), that sets forth facts concerning your operations and support to demonstrate that you are likely to satisfy the requirements to be classified as a private operating foundation; or (2) a statement describing your proposed operations as a private operating foundation? ☐ Yes ☐ No

5 If you answered "No" to line 1a, indicate the type of public charity status you are requesting by checking one of the choices below. You may check only one box.

The organization is not a private foundation because it is:

a 509(a)(1) and 170(b)(1)(A)(i)—a church or a convention or association of churches. Complete and attach Schedule A. ☐

b 509(a)(1) and 170(b)(1)(A)(ii)—a school. Complete and attach Schedule B. ☐

c 509(a)(1) and 170(b)(1)(A)(iii)—a hospital, a cooperative hospital service organization, or a medical research organization operated in conjunction with a hospital. Complete and attach Schedule C. ☐

d 509(a)(3)—an organization supporting either one or more organizations described in line 5a through c, f, g, or h or a publicly supported section 501(c)(4), (5), or (6) organization. Complete and attach Schedule D. ☐

Part X Public Charity Status (Continued)

e 509(a)(4)—an organization organized and operated exclusively for testing for public safety. ☐

f 509(a)(1) and 170(b)(1)(A)(iv)—an organization operated for the benefit of a college or university that is owned or operated by a governmental unit. ☐

g 509(a)(1) and 170(b)(1)(A)(vi)—an organization that receives a substantial part of its financial support in the form of contributions from publicly supported organizations, from a governmental unit, or from the general public. ☐

h 509(a)(2)—an organization that normally receives not more than one-third of its financial support from gross investment income and receives more than one-third of its financial support from contributions, membership fees, and gross receipts from activities related to its exempt functions (subject to certain exceptions). ☐

i A publicly supported organization, but unsure if it is described in 5g or 5h. The organization would like the IRS to decide the correct status. ☐

6 If you checked box g, h, or i in question 5 above, you must request either an advance or a definitive ruling by selecting one of the boxes below. Refer to the instructions to determine which type of ruling you are eligible to receive.

a Request for Advance Ruling: By checking this box and signing the consent, pursuant to section 6501(c)(4) of the Code you request an advance ruling and agree to extend the statute of limitations on the assessment of excise tax under section 4940 of the Code. The tax will apply only if you do not establish public support status at the end of the 5-year advance ruling period. The assessment period will be extended for the 5 advance ruling years to 8 years, 4 months, and 15 days beyond the end of the first year. You have the right to refuse or limit the extension to a mutually agreed-upon period of time or issue(s). Publication 1035, *Extending the Tax Assessment Period*, provides a more detailed explanation of your rights and the consequences of the choices you make. You may obtain Publication 1035 free of charge from the IRS web site at www.irs.gov or by calling toll-free 1-800-829-3676. Signing this consent will not deprive you of any appeal rights to which you would otherwise be entitled. If you decide not to extend the statute of limitations, you are not eligible for an advance ruling. ☐

Consent Fixing Period of Limitations Upon Assessment of Tax Under Section 4940 of the Internal Revenue Code

For Organization

(Signature of Officer, Director, Trustee, or other authorized official) (Type or print name of signer) (Date)

(Type or print title or authority of signer)

For IRS Use Only

IRS Director, Exempt Organizations (Date)

b Request for Definitive Ruling: Check this box if you have completed one tax year of at least 8 full months and you are requesting a definitive ruling. To confirm your public support status, answer line 6b(i) if you checked box g in line 5 above. Answer line 6b(ii) if you checked box h in line 5 above. If you checked box i in line 5 above, answer both lines 6b(i) and (ii). ☐

(i) (a) Enter 2% of line 8, column (e) on Part IX-A. Statement of Revenues and Expenses. ____________

(b) Attach a list showing the name and amount contributed by each person, company, or organization whose gifts totaled more than the 2% amount. If the answer is "None," check this box. ☐

(ii) (a) For each year amounts are included on lines 1, 2, and 9 of Part IX-A. Statement of Revenues and Expenses, attach a list showing the name of and amount received from each disqualified person. If the answer is "None," check this box. ☐

(b) For each year amounts are included on line 9 of Part IX-A. Statement of Revenues and Expenses, attach a list showing the name of and amount received from each payer, other than a disqualified person, whose payments were more than the larger of (1) 1% of line 10, Part IX-A. Statement of Revenues and Expenses, or (2) $5,000. If the answer is "None," check this box. ☐

7 Did you receive any unusual grants during any of the years shown on Part IX-A. Statement of Revenues and Expenses? If "Yes," attach a list including the name of the contributor, the date and amount of the grant, a brief description of the grant, and explain why it is unusual. ☐ Yes ☐ No

Part XI User Fee Information

You must include a user fee payment with this application. It will not be processed without your paid user fee. If your average annual gross receipts have exceeded or will exceed $10,000 annually over a 4-year period, you must submit payment of $750. If your gross receipts have not exceeded or will not exceed $10,000 annually over a 4-year period, the required user fee payment is $300. See instructions for Part XI, for a definition of gross receipts over a 4-year period. Your check or money order must be made payable to the United States Treasury. *User fees are subject to change. Check our website at www.irs.gov and type "User Fee" in the keyword box, or call Customer Account Services at 1-877-829-5500 for current information.*

1 Have your annual gross receipts averaged or are they expected to average not more than $10,000? ☐ Yes ☐ No
If "Yes," check the box on line 2 and enclose a user fee payment of $300 (Subject to change—see above).
If "No," check the box on line 3 and enclose a user fee payment of $750 (Subject to change—see above).

2 Check the box if you have enclosed the reduced user fee payment of $300 (Subject to change). ☐

3 Check the box if you have enclosed the user fee payment of $750 (Subject to change). ☐

I declare under the penalties of perjury that I am authorized to sign this application on behalf of the above organization and that I have examined this application, including the accompanying schedules and attachments, and to the best of my knowledge it is true, correct, and complete.

Please Sign Here ▶

(Signature of Officer, Director, Trustee, or other authorized official)	(Type or print name of signer)	(Date)
	(Type or print title or authority of signer)	

Reminder: Send the completed Form 1023 Checklist with your filled-in-application.

Schedule A. Churches

1a Do you have a written creed, statement of faith, or summary of beliefs? If "Yes," attach copies of relevant documents. ☐ Yes ☐ No

b Do you have a form of worship? If "Yes," describe your form of worship. ☐ Yes ☐ No

2a Do you have a formal code of doctrine and discipline? If "Yes," describe your code of doctrine and discipline. ☐ Yes ☐ No

b Do you have a distinct religious history? If "Yes," describe your religious history. ☐ Yes ☐ No

c Do you have a literature of your own? If "Yes," describe your literature. ☐ Yes ☐ No

3 Describe the organization's religious hierarchy or ecclesiastical government.

4a Do you have regularly scheduled religious services? If "Yes," describe the nature of the services and provide representative copies of relevant literature such as church bulletins. ☐ Yes ☐ No

b What is the average attendance at your regularly scheduled religious services? ____________

5a Do you have an established place of worship? If "Yes," refer to the instructions for the information required. ☐ Yes ☐ No

b Do you own the property where you have an established place of worship? ☐ Yes ☐ No

6 Do you have an established congregation or other regular membership group? If "No," refer to the instructions. ☐ Yes ☐ No

7 How many members do you have? ____________

8a Do you have a process by which an individual becomes a member? If "Yes," describe the process and complete lines 8b–8d, below. ☐ Yes ☐ No

b If you have members, do your members have voting rights, rights to participate in religious functions, or other rights? If "Yes," describe the rights your members have. ☐ Yes ☐ No

c May your members be associated with another denomination or church? ☐ Yes ☐ No

d Are all of your members part of the same family? ☐ Yes ☐ No

9 Do you conduct baptisms, weddings, funerals, etc.? ☐ Yes ☐ No

10 Do you have a school for the religious instruction of the young? ☐ Yes ☐ No

11a Do you have a minister or religious leader? If "Yes," describe this person's role and explain whether the minister or religious leader was ordained, commissioned, or licensed after a prescribed course of study. ☐ Yes ☐ No

b Do you have schools for the preparation of your ordained ministers or religious leaders? ☐ Yes ☐ No

12 Is your minister or religious leader also one of your officers, directors, or trustees? ☐ Yes ☐ No

13 Do you ordain, commission, or license ministers or religious leaders? If "Yes," describe the requirements for ordination, commission, or licensure. ☐ Yes ☐ No

14 Are you part of a group of churches with similar beliefs and structures? If "Yes," explain. Include the name of the group of churches. ☐ Yes ☐ No

15 Do you issue church charters? If "Yes," describe the requirements for issuing a charter. ☐ Yes ☐ No

16 Did you pay a fee for a church charter? If "Yes," attach a copy of the charter. ☐ Yes ☐ No

17 Do you have other information you believe should be considered regarding your status as a church? If "Yes," explain. ☐ Yes ☐ No

Schedule B. Schools, Colleges, and Universities

If you operate a school as an activity, complete Schedule B

Section I Operational Information

1a Do you normally have a regularly scheduled curriculum, a regular faculty of qualified teachers, a regularly enrolled student body, and facilities where your educational activities are regularly carried on? If "No," do not complete the remainder of Schedule B. ☐ Yes ☐ No

b Is the primary function of your school the presentation of formal instruction? If "Yes," describe your school in terms of whether it is an elementary, secondary, college, technical, or other type of school. If "No," do not complete the remainder of Schedule B. ☐ Yes ☐ No

2a Are you a public school because you are operated by a state or subdivision of a state? If "Yes," explain how you are operated by a state or subdivision of a state. Do not complete the remainder of Schedule B. ☐ Yes ☐ No

b Are you a public school because you are operated wholly or predominantly from government funds or property? If "Yes," explain how you are operated wholly or predominantly from government funds or property. Submit a copy of your funding agreement regarding government funding. Do not complete the remainder of Schedule B. ☐ Yes ☐ No

3 In what public school district, county, and state are you located?

4 Were you formed or substantially expanded at the time of public school desegregation in the above school district or county? ☐ Yes ☐ No

5 Has a state or federal administrative agency or judicial body ever determined that you are racially discriminatory? If "Yes," explain. ☐ Yes ☐ No

6 Has your right to receive financial aid or assistance from a governmental agency ever been revoked or suspended? If "Yes," explain. ☐ Yes ☐ No

7 Do you or will you contract with another organization to develop, build, market, or finance your facilities? If "Yes," explain how that entity is selected, explain how the terms of any contracts or other agreements are negotiated at arm's length, and explain how you determine that you will pay no more than fair market value for services. ☐ Yes ☐ No

Note. Make sure your answer is consistent with the information provided in Part VIII, line 7a.

8 Do you or will you manage your activities or facilities through your own employees or volunteers? If "No," attach a statement describing the activities that will be managed by others, the names of the persons or organizations that manage or will manage your activities or facilities, and how these managers were or will be selected. Also, submit copies of any contracts, proposed contracts, or other agreements regarding the provision of management services for your activities or facilities. Explain how the terms of any contracts or other agreements were or will be negotiated, and explain how you determine you will pay no more than fair market value for services. ☐ Yes ☐ No

Note. Answer "Yes" if you manage or intend to manage your programs through your own employees or by using volunteers. Answer "No" if you engage or intend to engage a separate organization or independent contractor. Make sure your answer is consistent with the information provided in Part VIII, line 7b.

Section II Establishment of Racially Nondiscriminatory Policy

Information required by Revenue Procedure 75-50.

1 Have you adopted a racially nondiscriminatory policy as to students in your organizing document, bylaws, or by resolution of your governing body? If "Yes," state where the policy can be found or supply a copy of the policy. If "No," you must adopt a nondiscriminatory policy as to students before submitting this application. See Publication 557. ☐ Yes ☐ No

2 Do your brochures, application forms, advertisements, and catalogues dealing with student admissions, programs, and scholarships contain a statement of your racially nondiscriminatory policy? ☐ Yes ☐ No

a If "Yes," attach a representative sample of each document.

b If "No," by checking the box to the right you agree that all future printed materials, including website content, will contain the required nondiscriminatory policy statement. ► ☐

3 Have you published a notice of your nondiscriminatory policy in a newspaper of general circulation that serves all racial segments of the community? (See the instructions for specific requirements.) If "No," explain. ☐ Yes ☐ No

4 Does or will the organization (or any department or division within it) discriminate in any way on the basis of race with respect to admissions; use of facilities or exercise of student privileges; faculty or administrative staff; or scholarship or loan programs? If "Yes," for any of the above, explain fully. ☐ Yes ☐ No

Schedule B. Schools, Colleges, and Universities (Continued)

5 Complete the table below to show the racial composition for the current academic year and projected for the next academic year, of: (a) the student body, (b) the faculty, and (c) the administrative staff. Provide actual numbers rather than percentages for each racial category.

If you are not operational, submit an estimate based on the best information available (such as the racial composition of the community served).

Racial Category	(a) Student Body		(b) Faculty		(c) Administrative Staff	
	Current Year	Next Year	Current Year	Next Year	Current Year	Next Year
Total						

6 In the table below, provide the number and amount of loans and scholarships awarded to students enrolled by racial categories.

Racial Category	Number of Loans		Amount of Loans		Number of Scholarships		Amount of Scholarships	
	Current Year	Next Year	Current Year	Next Year	Current Year	Next Year	Current Year	Next Year
Total								

7a Attach a list of your incorporators, founders, board members, and donors of land or buildings, whether individuals or organizations.

b Do any of these individuals or organizations have an objective to maintain segregated public or private school education? If "Yes," explain. ☐ Yes ☐ No

8 Will you maintain records according to the non-discrimination provisions contained in Revenue Procedure 75-50? If "No," explain. (See instructions.) ☐ Yes ☐ No

Schedule C. Hospitals and Medical Research Organizations

Check the box if you are a hospital. See the instructions for a definition of the term "hospital," which includes an organization whose principal purpose or function is providing hospital or medical care. Complete Section I below. ☐

Check the box if you are a medical research organization operated in conjunction with a hospital. See the instructions for a definition of the term "medical research organization," which refers to an organization whose principal purpose or function is medical research and which is directly engaged in the continuous active conduct of medical research in conjunction with a hospital. Complete Section II. ☐

Section I Hospitals

1a Are all the doctors in the community eligible for staff privileges? If "No," give the reasons why and explain how the medical staff is selected. ☐ Yes ☐ No

2a Do you or will you provide medical services to all individuals in your community who can pay for themselves or have private health insurance? If "No," explain. ☐ Yes ☐ No

b Do you or will you provide medical services to all individuals in your community who participate in Medicare? If "No," explain. ☐ Yes ☐ No

c Do you or will you provide medical services to all individuals in your community who participate in Medicaid? If "No," explain. ☐ Yes ☐ No

3a Do you or will you require persons covered by Medicare or Medicaid to pay a deposit before receiving services? If "Yes," explain. ☐ Yes ☐ No

b Does the same deposit requirement, if any, apply to all other patients? If "No," explain. ☐ Yes ☐ No

4a Do you or will you maintain a full-time emergency room? If "No," explain why you do not maintain a full-time emergency room. Also, describe any emergency services that you provide. ☐ Yes ☐ No

b Do you have a policy on providing emergency services to persons without apparent means to pay? If "Yes," provide a copy of the policy. ☐ Yes ☐ No

c Do you have any arrangements with police, fire, and voluntary ambulance services for the delivery or admission of emergency cases? If "Yes," describe the arrangements, including whether they are written or oral agreements. If written, submit copies of all such agreements. ☐ Yes ☐ No

5a Do you provide for a portion of your services and facilities to be used for charity patients? If "Yes," answer 5b through 5e. ☐ Yes ☐ No

b Explain your policy regarding charity cases, including how you distinguish between charity care and bad debts. Submit a copy of your written policy.

c Provide data on your past experience in admitting charity patients, including amounts you expend for treating charity care patients and types of services you provide to charity care patients.

d Describe any arrangements you have with federal, state, or local governments or government agencies for paying for the cost of treating charity care patients. Submit copies of any written agreements.

e Do you provide services on a sliding fee schedule depending on financial ability to pay? If "Yes," submit your sliding fee schedule. ☐ Yes ☐ No

6a Do you or will you carry on a formal program of medical training or medical research? If "Yes," describe such programs, including the type of programs offered, the scope of such programs, and affiliations with other hospitals or medical care providers with which you carry on the medical training or research programs. ☐ Yes ☐ No

b Do you or will you carry on a formal program of community education? If "Yes," describe such programs, including the type of programs offered, the scope of such programs, and affiliation with other hospitals or medical care providers with which you offer community education programs. ☐ Yes ☐ No

7 Do you or will you provide office space to physicians carrying on their own medical practices? If "Yes," describe the criteria for who may use the space, explain the means used to determine that you are paid at least fair market value, and submit representative lease agreements. ☐ Yes ☐ No

8 Is your board of directors comprised of a majority of individuals who are representative of the community you serve? Include a list of each board member's name and business, financial, or professional relationship with the hospital. Also, identify each board member who is representative of the community and describe how that individual is a community representative. ☐ Yes ☐ No

9 Do you participate in any joint ventures? If "Yes," state your ownership percentage in each joint venture, list your investment in each joint venture, describe the tax status of other participants in each joint venture (including whether they are section 501(c)(3) organizations), describe the activities of each joint venture, describe how you exercise control over the activities of each joint venture, and describe how each joint venture furthers your exempt purposes. Also, submit copies of all agreements. ☐ Yes ☐ No

Note. Make sure your answer is consistent with the information provided in Part VIII, line 8.

Schedule C. Hospitals and Medical Research Organizations (Continued)

Section I Hospitals (Continued)

10 Do you or will you manage your activities or facilities through your own employees or volunteers? If "No," attach a statement describing the activities that will be managed by others, the names of the persons or organizations that manage or will manage your activities or facilities, and how these managers were or will be selected. Also, submit copies of any contracts, proposed contracts, or other agreements regarding the provision of management services for your activities or facilities. Explain how the terms of any contracts or other agreements were or will be negotiated, and explain how you determine you will pay no more than fair market value for services. ☐ Yes ☐ No

Note. Answer "Yes" if you do manage or intend to manage your programs through your own employees or by using volunteers. Answer "No" if you engage or intend to engage a separate organization or independent contractor. Make sure your answer is consistent with the information provided in Part VIII, line 7b.

11 Do you or will you offer recruitment incentives to physicians? If "Yes," describe your recruitment incentives and attach copies of all written recruitment incentive policies. ☐ Yes ☐ No

12 Do you or will you lease equipment, assets, or office space from physicians who have a financial or professional relationship with you? If "Yes," explain how you establish a fair market value for the lease. ☐ Yes ☐ No

13 Have you purchased medical practices, ambulatory surgery centers, or other business assets from physicians or other persons with whom you have a business relationship, aside from the purchase? If "Yes," submit a copy of each purchase and sales contract and describe how you arrived at fair market value, including copies of appraisals. ☐ Yes ☐ No

14 Have you adopted a conflict of interest policy consistent with the sample health care organization conflict of interest policy in Appendix A of the instructions? If "Yes," submit a copy of the policy and explain how the policy has been adopted, such as by resolution of your governing board. If "No," explain how you will avoid any conflicts of interest in your business dealings. ☐ Yes ☐ No

Section II Medical Research Organizations

1 Name the hospitals with which you have a relationship and describe the relationship. Attach copies of written agreements with each hospital that demonstrate continuing relationships between you and the hospital(s).

2 Attach a schedule describing your present and proposed activities for the direct conduct of medical research; describe the nature of the activities, and the amount of money that has been or will be spent in carrying them out.

3 Attach a schedule of assets showing their fair market value and the portion of your assets directly devoted to medical research.

Schedule D. Section 509(a)(3) Supporting Organizations

Section I Identifying Information About the Supported Organization(s)

1 State the names, addresses, and EINs of the supported organizations. If additional space is needed, attach a separate sheet.

Name	Address	EIN
		–
		–

2 Are all supported organizations listed in line 1 public charities under section 509(a)(1) or (2)? If "Yes," go to Section II. If "No," go to line 3. ☐ Yes ☐ No

3 Do the supported organizations have tax-exempt status under section 501(c)(4), 501(c)(5), or 501(c)(6)? ☐ Yes ☐ No

If "Yes," for each 501(c)(4), (5), or (6) organization supported, provide the following financial information:

- Part IX-A. Statement of Revenues and Expenses, lines 1–13 and
- Part X, lines 6b(ii)(a), 6b(ii)(b), and 7.

If "No," attach a statement describing how each organization you support is a public charity under section 509(a)(1) or (2).

Section II Relationship with Supported Organization(s)—Three Tests

To be classified as a supporting organization, an organization must meet one of three relationship tests:

Test 1: "Operated, supervised, or controlled by" one or more publicly supported organizations, or

Test 2: "Supervised or controlled in connection with" one or more publicly supported organizations, or

Test 3: "Operated in connection with" one or more publicly supported organizations.

1 Information to establish the "operated, supervised, or controlled by" relationship (Test 1)

Is a majority of your governing board or officers elected or appointed by the supported organization(s)? If "Yes," describe the process by which your governing board is appointed and elected; go to Section III. If "No," continue to line 2. ☐ Yes ☐ No

2 Information to establish the "supervised or controlled in connection with" relationship (Test 2)

Does a majority of your governing board consist of individuals who also serve on the governing board of the supported organization(s)? If "Yes," describe the process by which your governing board is appointed and elected; go to Section III. If "No," go to line 3. ☐ Yes ☐ No

3 Information to establish the "operated in connection with" responsiveness test (Test 3)

Are you a trust from which the named supported organization(s) can enforce and compel an accounting under state law? If "Yes," explain whether you advised the supported organization(s) in writing of these rights and provide a copy of the written communication documenting this; go to Section II, line 5. If "No," go to line 4a. ☐ Yes ☐ No

4 Information to establish the alternative "operated in connection with" responsiveness test (Test 3)

a Do the officers, directors, trustees, or members of the supported organization(s) elect or appoint one or more of your officers, directors, or trustees? If "Yes," explain and provide documentation; go to line 4d, below. If "No," go to line 4b. ☐ Yes ☐ No

b Do one or more members of the governing body of the supported organization(s) also serve as your officers, directors, or trustees or hold other important offices with respect to you? If "Yes," explain and provide documentation; go to line 4d, below. If "No," go to line 4c. ☐ Yes ☐ No

c Do your officers, directors, or trustees maintain a close and continuous working relationship with the officers, directors, or trustees of the supported organization(s)? If "Yes," explain and provide documentation. ☐ Yes ☐ No

d Do the supported organization(s) have a significant voice in your investment policies, in the making and timing of grants, and in otherwise directing the use of your income or assets? If "Yes," explain and provide documentation. ☐ Yes ☐ No

e Describe and provide copies of written communications documenting how you made the supported organization(s) aware of your supporting activities.

Schedule D. Section 509(a)(3) Supporting Organizations (Continued)

Section II Relationship with Supported Organization(s)—Three Tests (Continued)

5 Information to establish the "operated in connection with" integral part test (Test 3)
Do you conduct activities that would otherwise be carried out by the supported organization(s)? If "Yes," explain and go to Section III. If "No," continue to line 6a. ☐ Yes ☐ No

6 Information to establish the alternative "operated in connection with" integral part test (Test 3)

a Do you distribute at least 85% of your annual net income to the supported organization(s)? If "Yes," go to line 6b. (See instructions.) ☐ Yes ☐ No

If "No," state the percentage of your income that you distribute to each supported organization. Also explain how you ensure that the supported organization(s) are attentive to your operations.

b How much do you contribute annually to each supported organization? Attach a schedule.

c What is the total annual revenue of each supported organization? If you need additional space, attach a list.

d Do you or the supported organization(s) earmark your funds for support of a particular program or activity? If "Yes," explain. ☐ Yes ☐ No

7a Does your organizing document specify the supported organization(s) by name? If "Yes," state the article and paragraph number and go to Section III. If "No," answer line 7b. ☐ Yes ☐ No

b Attach a statement describing whether there has been an historic and continuing relationship between you and the supported organization(s).

Section III Organizational Test

1a If you met relationship Test 1 or Test 2 in Section II, your organizing document must specify the supported organization(s) by name, or by naming a similar purpose or charitable class of beneficiaries. If your organizing document complies with this requirement, answer "Yes." If your organizing document does not comply with this requirement, answer "No," and see the instructions. ☐ Yes ☐ No

b If you met relationship Test 3 in Section II, your organizing document must generally specify the supported organization(s) by name. If your organizing document complies with this requirement, answer "Yes," and go to Section IV. If your organizing document does not comply with this requirement, answer "No," and see the instructions. ☐ Yes ☐ No

Section IV Disqualified Person Test

You do not qualify as a supporting organization if you are controlled directly or indirectly by one or more disqualified persons (as defined in section 4946) other than foundation managers or one or more organizations that you support. Foundation managers who are also disqualified persons for another reason are disqualified persons with respect to you.

1a Do any persons who are disqualified persons with respect to you, (except individuals who are disqualified persons only because they are foundation managers), appoint any of your foundation managers? If "Yes," (1) describe the process by which disqualified persons appoint any of your foundation managers, (2) provide the names of these disqualified persons and the foundation managers they appoint, and (3) explain how control is vested over your operations (including assets and activities) by persons other than disqualified persons. ☐ Yes ☐ No

b Do any persons who have a family or business relationship with any disqualified persons with respect to you, (except individuals who are disqualified persons only because they are foundation managers), appoint any of your foundation managers? If "Yes," (1) describe the process by which individuals with a family or business relationship with disqualified persons appoint any of your foundation managers, (2) provide the names of these disqualified persons, the individuals with a family or business relationship with disqualified persons, and the foundation managers appointed, and (3) explain how control is vested over your operations (including assets and activities) in individuals other than disqualified persons. ☐ Yes ☐ No

c Do any persons who are disqualified persons, (except individuals who are disqualified persons only because they are foundation managers), have any influence regarding your operations, including your assets or activities? If "Yes," (1) provide the names of these disqualified persons, (2) explain how influence is exerted over your operations (including assets and activities), and (3) explain how control is vested over your operations (including assets and activities) by individuals other than disqualified persons. ☐ Yes ☐ No

Schedule E. Organizations Not Filing Form 1023 Within 27 Months of Formation

Schedule E is intended to determine whether you are eligible for tax exemption under section 501(c)(3) from the postmark date of your application or from your date of incorporation or formation, whichever is earlier. If you are not eligible for tax exemption under section 501(c)(3) from your date of incorporation or formation, Schedule E is also intended to determine whether you are eligible for tax exemption under section 501(c)(4) for the period between your date of incorporation or formation and the postmark date of your application.

1 Are you a church, association of churches, or integrated auxiliary of a church? If "Yes," complete Schedule A and stop here. Do not complete the remainder of Schedule E. ☐ Yes ☐ No

2a Are you a public charity with annual gross receipts that are normally $5,000 or less? If "Yes," stop here. Answer "No" if you are a private foundation, regardless of your gross receipts. ☐ Yes ☐ No

b If your gross receipts were normally more than $5,000, are you filing this application within 90 days from the end of the tax year in which your gross receipts were normally more than $5,000? If "Yes," stop here. ☐ Yes ☐ No

3a Were you included as a subordinate in a group exemption application or letter? If "No," go to line 4. ☐ Yes ☐ No

b If you were included as a subordinate in a group exemption letter, are you filing this application within 27 months from the date you were notified by the organization holding the group exemption letter or the Internal Revenue Service that you cease to be covered by the group exemption letter? If "Yes," stop here. ☐ Yes ☐ No

c If you were included as a subordinate in a timely filed group exemption request that was denied, are you filing this application within 27 months from the postmark date of the Internal Revenue Service final adverse ruling letter? If "Yes," stop here. ☐ Yes ☐ No

4 Were you created on or before October 9, 1969? If "Yes," stop here. Do not complete the remainder of this schedule. ☐ Yes ☐ No

5 If you answered "No" to lines 1 through 4, we cannot recognize you as tax exempt from your date of formation unless you qualify for an extension of time to apply for exemption. Do you wish to request an extension of time to apply to be recognized as exempt from the date you were formed? If "Yes," attach a statement explaining why you did not file this application within the 27-month period. Do not answer lines 6, 7, or 8. If "No," go to line 6a. ☐ Yes ☐ No

6a If you answered "No" to line 5, you can only be exempt under section 501(c)(3) from the postmark date of this application. Therefore, do you want us to treat this application as a request for tax exemption from the postmark date? If "Yes," you are eligible for an advance ruling. Complete Part X, line 6a. If "No," you will be treated as a private foundation. ☐ Yes ☐ No

Note. Be sure your ruling eligibility agrees with your answer to Part X, line 6.

b Do you anticipate significant changes in your sources of support in the future? If "Yes," complete line 7 below. ☐ Yes ☐ No

Schedule E. Organizations Not Filing Form 1023 Within 27 Months of Formation *(Continued)*

7 Complete this item only if you answered "Yes" to line 6b. Include projected revenue for the first two full years following the current tax year.

Type of Revenue	Projected revenue for 2 years following current tax year		
	(a) From .... To	(b) From .... To	(c) Total
1 Gifts, grants, and contributions received (do not include unusual grants)			
2 Membership fees received			
3 Gross investment income			
4 Net unrelated business income			
5 Taxes levied for your benefit			
6 Value of services or facilities furnished by a governmental unit without charge (not including the value of services generally furnished to the public without charge)			
7 Any revenue not otherwise listed above or in lines 9–12 below (attach an itemized list)			
8 Total of lines 1 through 7			
9 Gross receipts from admissions, merchandise sold, or services performed, or furnishing of facilities in any activity that is related to your exempt purposes (attach itemized list)			
10 Total of lines 8 and 9			
11 Net gain or loss on sale of capital assets (attach an itemized list)			
12 Unusual grants			
13 Total revenue. Add lines 10 through 12			

8 According to your answers, you are only eligible for tax exemption under section 501(c)(3) from the postmark date of your application. However, you may be eligible for tax exemption under section 501(c)(4) from your date of formation to the postmark date of the Form 1023. Tax exemption under section 501(c)(4) allows exemption from federal income tax, but generally not deductibility of contributions under Code section 170. Check the box at right if you want us to treat this as a request for exemption under 501(c)(4) from your date of formation to the postmark date. ▶ ☐

Attach a completed Page 1 of Form 1024, Application for Recognition of Exemption Under Section 501(a), to this application.

Schedule F. Homes for the Elderly or Handicapped and Low-Income Housing

Section I General Information About Your Housing

1 Describe the type of housing you provide.

2 Provide copies of any application forms you use for admission.

3 Explain how the public is made aware of your facility.

4a Provide a description of each facility.
 b What is the total number of residents each facility can accommodate?
 c What is your current number of residents in each facility?
 d Describe each facility in terms of whether residents rent or purchase housing from you.

5 Attach a sample copy of your residency or homeownership contract or agreement.

6 Do you participate in any joint ventures? If "Yes," state your ownership percentage in each joint venture, list your investment in each joint venture, describe the tax status of other participants in each joint venture (including whether they are section 501(c)(3) organizations), describe the activities of each joint venture, describe how you exercise control over the activities of each joint venture, and describe how each joint venture furthers your exempt purpose. Also, submit copies of all joint venture agreements. ☐ Yes ☐ No

Note. Make sure your answer is consistent with the information provided in Part VIII, line 8.

7 Do you or will you contract with another organization to develop, build, market, or finance your housing? If "Yes," explain how that entity is selected, explain how the terms of any contract(s) are negotiated at arm's length, and explain how you determine you will pay no more than fair market value for services. ☐ Yes ☐ No

Note. Make sure your answer is consistent with the information provided in Part VIII, line 7a.

8 Do you or will you manage your activities or facilities through your own employees or volunteers? If "No," attach a statement describing the activities that will be managed by others, the names of the persons or organizations that manage or will manage your activities or facilities, and how these managers were or will be selected. Also, submit copies of any contracts, proposed contracts, or other agreements regarding the provision of management services for your activities or facilities. Explain how the terms of any contracts or other agreements were or will be negotiated, and explain how you determine you will pay no more than fair market value for services. ☐ Yes ☐ No

Note. Answer "Yes" if you do manage or intend to manage your programs through your own employees or by using volunteers. Answer "No" if you engage or intend to engage a separate organization or independent contractor. Make sure your answer is consistent with the information provided in Part VIII, line 7b.

9 Do you participate in any government housing programs? If "Yes," describe these programs. ☐ Yes ☐ No

10a Do you own the facility? If "No," describe any enforceable rights you possess to purchase the facility in the future; go to line 10c. If "Yes," answer line 10b. ☐ Yes ☐ No

 b How did you acquire the facility? For example, did you develop it yourself, purchase a project, etc. Attach all contracts, transfer agreements, or other documents connected with the acquisition of the facility.

 c Do you lease the facility or the land on which it is located? If "Yes," describe the parties to the lease(s) and provide copies of all leases. ☐ Yes ☐ No

Schedule F. Homes for the Elderly or Handicapped and Low-Income Housing *(Continued)*

Section II Homes for the Elderly or Handicapped

1a Do you provide housing for the elderly? If "Yes," describe who qualifies for your housing in terms of age, infirmity, or other criteria and explain how you select persons for your housing. ☐ Yes ☐ No

b Do you provide housing for the handicapped? If "Yes," describe who qualifies for your housing in terms of disability, income levels, or other criteria and explain how you select persons for your housing. ☐ Yes ☐ No

2a Do you charge an entrance or founder's fee? If "Yes," describe what this charge covers, whether it is a one-time fee, how the fee is determined, whether it is payable in a lump sum or on an installment basis, whether it is refundable, and the circumstances, if any, under which it may be waived. ☐ Yes ☐ No

b Do you charge periodic fees or maintenance charges? If "Yes," describe what these charges cover and how they are determined. ☐ Yes ☐ No

c Is your housing affordable to a significant segment of the elderly or handicapped persons in the community? Identify your community. Also, if "Yes," explain how you determine your housing is affordable. ☐ Yes ☐ No

3a Do you have an established policy concerning residents who become unable to pay their regular charges? If "Yes," describe your established policy. ☐ Yes ☐ No

b Do you have any arrangements with government welfare agencies or others to absorb all or part of the cost of maintaining residents who become unable to pay their regular charges? If "Yes," describe these arrangements. ☐ Yes ☐ No

4 Do you have arrangements for the healthcare needs of your residents? If "Yes," describe these arrangements. ☐ Yes ☐ No

5 Are your facilities designed to meet the physical, emotional, recreational, social, religious, and/or other similar needs of the elderly or handicapped? If "Yes," describe these design features. ☐ Yes ☐ No

Section III Low-Income Housing

1 Do you provide low-income housing? If "Yes," describe who qualifies for your housing in terms of income levels or other criteria, and describe how you select persons for your housing. ☐ Yes ☐ No

2 In addition to rent or mortgage payments, do residents pay periodic fees or maintenance charges? If "Yes," describe what these charges cover and how they are determined. ☐ Yes ☐ No

3a Is your housing affordable to low income residents? If "Yes," describe how your housing is made affordable to low-income residents. ☐ Yes ☐ No

Note. Revenue Procedure 96-32, 1996-1 C.B. 717, provides guidelines for providing low-income housing that will be treated as charitable. (At least 75% of the units are occupied by low-income tenants or 40% are occupied by tenants earning not more than 120% of the very low-income levels for the area.)

b Do you impose any restrictions to make sure that your housing remains affordable to low-income residents? If "Yes," describe these restrictions. ☐ Yes ☐ No

4 Do you provide social services to residents? If "Yes," describe these services. ☐ Yes ☐ No

Schedule G. Successors to Other Organizations

1a Are you a successor to a for-profit organization? If "Yes," explain the relationship with the predecessor organization that resulted in your creation and complete line 1b. ☐ Yes ☐ No

b Explain why you took over the activities or assets of a for-profit organization or converted from for-profit to nonprofit status.

2a Are you a successor to an organization other than a for-profit organization? Answer "Yes" if you have taken or will take over the activities of another organization; or you have taken or will take over 25% or more of the fair market value of the net assets of another organization. If "Yes," explain the relationship with the other organization that resulted in your creation. ☐ Yes ☐ No

b Provide the tax status of the predecessor organization.

c Did you or did an organization to which you are a successor previously apply for tax exemption under section 501(c)(3) or any other section of the Code? If "Yes," explain how the application was resolved. ☐ Yes ☐ No

d Was your prior tax exemption or the tax exemption of an organization to which you are a successor revoked or suspended? If "Yes," explain. Include a description of the corrections you made to re-establish tax exemption. ☐ Yes ☐ No

e Explain why you took over the activities or assets of another organization.

3 Provide the name, last address, and EIN of the predecessor organization and describe its activities.

Name: ______________________ EIN: ___–___

Address: ______________________

4 List the owners, partners, principal stockholders, officers, and governing board members of the predecessor organization. Attach a separate sheet if additional space is needed.

Name	Address	Share/Interest (If a for-profit)

5 Do or will any of the persons listed in line 4, maintain a working relationship with you? If "Yes," describe the relationship in detail and include copies of any agreements with any of these persons or with any for-profit organizations in which these persons own more than a 35% interest. ☐ Yes ☐ No

6a Were any assets transferred, whether by gift or sale, from the predecessor organization to you? ☐ Yes ☐ No
If "Yes," provide a list of assets, indicate the value of each asset, explain how the value was determined, and attach an appraisal, if available. For each asset listed, also explain if the transfer was by gift, sale, or combination thereof.

b Were any restrictions placed on the use or sale of the assets? If "Yes," explain the restrictions. ☐ Yes ☐ No

c Provide a copy of the agreement(s) of sale or transfer.

7 Were any debts or liabilities transferred from the predecessor for-profit organization to you? ☐ Yes ☐ No
If "Yes," provide a list of the debts or liabilities that were transferred to you, indicating the amount of each, how the amount was determined, and the name of the person to whom the debt or liability is owed.

8 Will you lease or rent any property or equipment previously owned or used by the predecessor for-profit organization, or from persons listed in line 4, or from for-profit organizations in which these persons own more than a 35% interest? If "Yes," submit a copy of the lease or rental agreement(s). Indicate how the lease or rental value of the property or equipment was determined. ☐ Yes ☐ No

9 Will you lease or rent property or equipment to persons listed in line 4, or to for-profit organizations in which these persons own more than a 35% interest? If "Yes," attach a list of the property or equipment, provide a copy of the lease or rental agreement(s), and indicate how the lease or rental value of the property or equipment was determined. ☐ Yes ☐ No

Schedule H. Organizations Providing Scholarships, Fellowships, Educational Loans, or Other Educational Grants to Individuals and Private Foundations Requesting Advance Approval of Individual Grant Procedures

Section I *Names of individual recipients are not required to be listed in Schedule H.*
Public charities and private foundations complete lines 1a through 7 of this section. See the instructions to Part X if you are not sure whether you are a public charity or a private foundation.

1a Describe the types of educational grants you provide to individuals, such as scholarships, fellowships, loans, etc.
b Describe the purpose and amount of your scholarships, fellowships, and other educational grants and loans that you award.
c If you award educational loans, explain the terms of the loans (interest rate, length, forgiveness, etc.).
d Specify how your program is publicized.
e Provide copies of any solicitation or announcement materials.
f Provide a sample copy of the application used.

2 Do you maintain case histories showing recipients of your scholarships, fellowships, educational loans, or other educational grants, including names, addresses, purposes of awards, amount of each grant, manner of selection, and relationship (if any) to officers, trustees, or donors of funds to you? If "No," refer to the instructions. ☐ Yes ☐ No

3 Describe the specific criteria you use to determine who is eligible for your program. (For example, eligibility selection criteria could consist of graduating high school students from a particular high school who will attend college, writers of scholarly works about American history, etc.)

4a Describe the specific criteria you use to select recipients. (For example, specific selection criteria could consist of prior academic performance, financial need, etc.)
b Describe how you determine the number of grants that will be made annually.
c Describe how you determine the amount of each of your grants.
d Describe any requirement or condition that you impose on recipients to obtain, maintain, or qualify for renewal of a grant. (For example, specific requirements or conditions could consist of attendance at a four-year college, maintaining a certain grade point average, teaching in public school after graduation from college, etc.)

5 Describe your procedures for supervising the scholarships, fellowships, educational loans, or other educational grants. Describe whether you obtain reports and grade transcripts from recipients, or you pay grants directly to a school under an arrangement whereby the school will apply the grant funds only for enrolled students who are in good standing. Also, describe your procedures for taking action if the terms of the award are violated.

6 Who is on the selection committee for the awards made under your program, including names of current committee members, criteria for committee membership, and the method of replacing committee members?

7 Are relatives of members of the selection committee, or of your officers, directors, or substantial contributors eligible for awards made under your program? If "Yes," what measures are taken to ensure unbiased selections? ☐ Yes ☐ No

Note. If you are a private foundation, you are not permitted to provide educational grants to disqualified persons. Disqualified persons include your substantial contributors and foundation managers and certain family members of disqualified persons.

Section II **Private foundations complete lines 1a through 4f of this section. Public charities do not complete this section.**

1a If we determine that you are a private foundation, do you want this application to be considered as a request for advance approval of grant making procedures? ☐ Yes ☐ No ☐ N/A
b For which section(s) do you wish to be considered?
- 4945(g)(1)—Scholarship or fellowship grant to an individual for study at an educational institution ☐
- 4945(g)(3)—Other grants, including loans, to an individual for travel, study, or other similar purposes, to enhance a particular skill of the grantee or to produce a specific product ☐

2 Do you represent that you will (1) arrange to receive and review grantee reports annually and upon completion of the purpose for which the grant was awarded, (2) investigate diversions of funds from their intended purposes, and (3) take all reasonable and appropriate steps to recover diverted funds, ensure other grant funds held by a grantee are used for their intended purposes, and withhold further payments to grantees until you obtain grantees' assurances that future diversions will not occur and that grantees will take extraordinary precautions to prevent future diversions from occurring? ☐ Yes ☐ No

3 Do you represent that you will maintain all records relating to individual grants, including information obtained to evaluate grantees, identify whether a grantee is a disqualified person, establish the amount and purpose of each grant, and establish that you undertook the supervision and investigation of grants described in line 2? ☐ Yes ☐ No

Schedule H. Organizations Providing Scholarships, Fellowships, Educational Loans, or Other Educational Grants to Individuals and Private Foundations Requesting Advance Approval of Individual Grant Procedures (Continued)

Section II Private foundations complete lines 1a through 4f of this section. Public charities do not complete this section. (Continued)

4a Do you or will you award scholarships, fellowships, and educational loans to attend an educational institution based on the status of an individual being an employee of a particular employer? If "Yes," complete lines 4b through 4f. ☐ Yes ☐ No

b Will you comply with the seven conditions and either the percentage tests or facts and circumstances test for scholarships, fellowships, and educational loans to attend an educational institution as set forth in Revenue Procedures 76-47, 1976-2 C.B. 670, and 80-39, 1980-2 C.B. 772, which apply to inducement, selection committee, eligibility requirements, objective basis of selection, employment, course of study, and other objectives? (See lines 4c, 4d, and 4e, regarding the percentage tests.) ☐ Yes ☐ No

c Do you or will you provide scholarships, fellowships, or educational loans to attend an educational institution to employees of a particular employer? ☐ Yes ☐ No ☐ N/A

If "Yes," will you award grants to 10% or fewer of the eligible applicants who were actually considered by the selection committee in selecting recipients of grants in that year as provided by Revenue Procedures 76-47 and 80-39? ☐ Yes ☐ No

d Do you provide scholarships, fellowships, or educational loans to attend an educational institution to children of employees of a particular employer? ☐ Yes ☐ No ☐ N/A

If "Yes," will you award grants to 25% or fewer of the eligible applicants who were actually considered by the selection committee in selecting recipients of grants in that year as provided by Revenue Procedures 76-47 and 80-39? If "No," go to line 4e. ☐ Yes ☐ No

e If you provide scholarships, fellowships, or educational loans to attend an educational institution to children of employees of a particular employer, will you award grants to 10% or fewer of the number of employees' children who can be shown to be eligible for grants (whether or not they submitted an application) in that year, as provided by Revenue Procedures 76-47 and 80-39? ☐ Yes ☐ No ☐ N/A

If "Yes," describe how you will determine who can be shown to be eligible for grants without submitting an application, such as by obtaining written statements or other information about the expectations of employees' children to attend an educational institution. If "No," go to line 4f.

Note. Statistical or sampling techniques are not acceptable. See Revenue Procedure 85-51, 1985-2 C.B. 717, for additional information.

f If you provide scholarships, fellowships, or educational loans to attend an educational institution to children of employees of a particular employer without regard to either the 25% limitation described in line 4d, or the 10% limitation described in line 4e, will you award grants based on facts and circumstances that demonstrate that the grants will not be considered compensation for past, present, or future services or otherwise provide a significant benefit to the particular employer? If "Yes," describe the facts and circumstances that you believe will demonstrate that the grants are neither compensatory nor a significant benefit to the particular employer. In your explanation, describe why you cannot satisfy either the 25% test described in line 4d or the 10% test described in line 4e. ☐ Yes ☐ No

Form 1040 Department of the Treasury—Internal Revenue Service
U.S. Individual Income Tax Return 2006

(99) IRS Use Only—Do not write or staple in this space.

For the year Jan. 1–Dec. 31, 2006, or other tax year beginning , 2006, ending , 20 OMB No. 1545-0074

Label (See instructions on page 16.) Use the IRS label. Otherwise, please print or type. LABEL HERE

Your first name and initial | Last name | Your social security number

If a joint return, spouse's first name and initial | Last name | Spouse's social security number

Home address (number and street). If you have a P.O. box, see page 16. | Apt. no. | ▲ You must enter your SSN(s) above. ▲

City, town or post office, state, and ZIP code. If you have a foreign address, see page 16. | Checking a box below will not change your tax or refund.

Presidential Election Campaign ▶ Check here if you, or your spouse if filing jointly, want $3 to go to this fund (see page 16) ▶ ☐ You ☐ Spouse

Filing Status

Check only one box.

1 ☐ Single
2 ☐ Married filing jointly (even if only one had income)
3 ☐ Married filing separately. Enter spouse's SSN above and full name here. ▶
4 ☐ Head of household (with qualifying person). (See page 17.) If the qualifying person is a child but not your dependent, enter this child's name here. ▶
5 ☐ Qualifying widow(er) with dependent child (see page 17)

Exemptions

6a ☐ **Yourself.** If someone can claim you as a dependent, do not check box 6a
b ☐ **Spouse**
c **Dependents:**

(1) First name Last name	(2) Dependent's social security number	(3) Dependent's relationship to you	(4) ✓ if qualifying child for child tax credit (see page 19)
			☐
			☐
			☐
			☐

If more than four dependents, see page 19.

d Total number of exemptions claimed

Boxes checked on 6a and 6b ____
No. of children on 6c who:
• lived with you ____
• did not live with you due to divorce or separation (see page 20) ____
Dependents on 6c not entered above ____
Add numbers on lines above ▶

Income

Attach Form(s) W-2 here. Also attach Forms W-2G and 1099-R if tax was withheld.

If you did not get a W-2, see page 23.

Enclose, but do not attach, any payment. Also, please use Form 1040-V.

7 Wages, salaries, tips, etc. Attach Form(s) W-2 — 7
8a **Taxable** interest. Attach Schedule B if required — 8a
b **Tax-exempt** interest. Do not include on line 8a — 8b
9a Ordinary dividends. Attach Schedule B if required — 9a
b Qualified dividends (see page 23) — 9b
10 Taxable refunds, credits, or offsets of state and local income taxes (see page 24) — 10
11 Alimony received — 11
12 Business income or (loss). Attach Schedule C or C-EZ — 12
13 Capital gain or (loss). Attach Schedule D if required. If not required, check here ▶ ☐ — 13
14 Other gains or (losses). Attach Form 4797 — 14
15a IRA distributions 15a — b Taxable amount (see page 25) — 15b
16a Pensions and annuities 16a — b Taxable amount (see page 26) — 16b
17 Rental real estate, royalties, partnerships, S corporations, trusts, etc. Attach Schedule E — 17
18 Farm income or (loss). Attach Schedule F — 18
19 Unemployment compensation — 19
20a Social security benefits 20a — b Taxable amount (see page 27) — 20b
21 Other income. List type and amount (see page 29) — 21
22 Add the amounts in the far right column for lines 7 through 21. This is your **total income** ▶ 22

Adjusted Gross Income

23 Archer MSA deduction. Attach Form 8853 — 23
24 Certain business expenses of reservists, performing artists, and fee-basis government officials. Attach Form 2106 or 2106-EZ — 24
25 Health savings account deduction. Attach Form 8889 — 25
26 Moving expenses. Attach Form 3903 — 26
27 One-half of self-employment tax. Attach Schedule SE — 27
28 Self-employed SEP, SIMPLE, and qualified plans — 28
29 Self-employed health insurance deduction (see page 29) — 29
30 Penalty on early withdrawal of savings — 30
31a Alimony paid b Recipient's SSN ▶ — 31a
32 IRA deduction (see page 31) — 32
33 Student loan interest deduction (see page 33) — 33
34 Jury duty pay you gave to your employer — 34
35 Domestic production activities deduction. Attach Form 8903 — 35
36 Add lines 23 through 31a and 32 through 35 — 36
37 Subtract line 36 from line 22. This is your **adjusted gross income** ▶ 37

For Disclosure, Privacy Act, and Paperwork Reduction Act Notice, see page 80. Cat. No. 11320B Form **1040** (2006)

Form 1040 (2006) Page 2

Tax and Credits

Standard Deduction for— • People who checked any box on line 39a or 39b or who can be claimed as a dependent, see page 34. • All others: Single or Married filing separately, $5,150 Married filing jointly or Qualifying widow(er), $10,300 Head of household, $7,550

- 38 Amount from line 37 (adjusted gross income) — 38
- 39a Check if: ☐ You were born before January 2, 1942, ☐ Blind. ☐ Spouse was born before January 2, 1942, ☐ Blind. Total boxes checked ▶ 39a
- b If your spouse itemizes on a separate return or you were a dual-status alien, see page 34 and check here ▶39b ☐
- 40 Itemized deductions (from Schedule A) or your standard deduction (see left margin) — 40
- 41 Subtract line 40 from line 38 — 41
- 42 If line 38 is over $112,875, or you provided housing to a person displaced by Hurricane Katrina, see page 36. Otherwise, multiply $3,300 by the total number of exemptions claimed on line 6d — 42
- 43 Taxable income. Subtract line 42 from line 41. If line 42 is more than line 41, enter -0- — 43
- 44 Tax (see page 36). Check if any tax is from: a ☐ Form(s) 8814 b ☐ Form 4972 — 44
- 45 Alternative minimum tax (see page 39). Attach Form 6251 — 45
- 46 Add lines 44 and 45 ▶ 46
- 47 Foreign tax credit. Attach Form 1116 if required — 47
- 48 Credit for child and dependent care expenses. Attach Form 2441 — 48
- 49 Credit for the elderly or the disabled. Attach Schedule R — 49
- 50 Education credits. Attach Form 8863 — 50
- 51 Retirement savings contributions credit. Attach Form 8880 — 51
- 52 Residential energy credits. Attach Form 5695 — 52
- 53 Child tax credit (see page 42). Attach Form 8901 if required — 53
- 54 Credits from: a ☐ Form 8396 b ☐ Form 8839 c ☐ Form 8859 — 54
- 55 Other credits: a ☐ Form 3800 b ☐ Form 8801 c ☐ Form ____ — 55
- 56 Add lines 47 through 55. These are your total credits — 56
- 57 Subtract line 56 from line 46. If line 56 is more than line 46, enter -0- ▶ 57

Other Taxes

- 58 Self-employment tax. Attach Schedule SE — 58
- 59 Social security and Medicare tax on tip income not reported to employer. Attach Form 4137 — 59
- 60 Additional tax on IRAs, other qualified retirement plans, etc. Attach Form 5329 if required — 60
- 61 Advance earned income credit payments from Form(s) W-2, box 9 — 61
- 62 Household employment taxes. Attach Schedule H — 62
- 63 Add lines 57 through 62. This is your total tax ▶ 63

Payments

If you have a qualifying child, attach Schedule EIC.

- 64 Federal income tax withheld from Forms W-2 and 1099 — 64
- 65 2006 estimated tax payments and amount applied from 2005 return — 65
- 66a Earned income credit (EIC) — 66a
- b Nontaxable combat pay election ▶ 66b
- 67 Excess social security and tier 1 RRTA tax withheld (see page 60) — 67
- 68 Additional child tax credit. Attach Form 8812 — 68
- 69 Amount paid with request for extension to file (see page 60) — 69
- 70 Payments from: a ☐ Form 2439 b ☐ Form 4136 c ☐ Form 8885 — 70
- 71 Credit for federal telephone excise tax paid. Attach Form 8913 if required — 71
- 72 Add lines 64, 65, 66a, and 67 through 71. These are your total payments ▶ 72

Refund

Direct deposit? See page 61 and fill in 74b, 74c, and 74d, or Form 8888.

- 73 If line 72 is more than line 63, subtract line 63 from line 72. This is the amount you overpaid — 73
- 74a Amount of line 73 you want refunded to you. If Form 8888 is attached, check here ▶ ☐ — 74a
- ▶ b Routing number ▶ c Type: ☐ Checking ☐ Savings
- ▶ d Account number
- 75 Amount of line 73 you want applied to your 2007 estimated tax ▶ 75

Amount You Owe

- 76 Amount you owe. Subtract line 72 from line 63. For details on how to pay, see page 62 ▶ 76
- 77 Estimated tax penalty (see page 62) — 77

Third Party Designee

Do you want to allow another person to discuss this return with the IRS (see page 63)? ☐ Yes. Complete the following. ☐ No

Designee's name ▶ Phone no. ▶ ( ) Personal identification number (PIN) ▶

Sign Here

Joint return? See page 17. Keep a copy for your records.

Under penalties of perjury, I declare that I have examined this return and accompanying schedules and statements, and to the best of my knowledge and belief, they are true, correct, and complete. Declaration of preparer (other than taxpayer) is based on all information of which preparer has any knowledge.

Your signature	Date	Your occupation	Daytime phone number
			( )
Spouse's signature. If a joint return, both must sign.	Date	Spouse's occupation	

Paid Preparer's Use Only

Preparer's signature ▶	Date	Check if self-employed ☐	Preparer's SSN or PTIN
Firm's name (or yours if self-employed), address, and ZIP code ▶		EIN	
		Phone no. ( )	

Form 1040 (2006)

SCHEDULES A&B (Form 1040)

Department of the Treasury Internal Revenue Service (99)

Schedule A—Itemized Deductions

(Schedule B is on back)

▶ Attach to Form 1040. ▶ See Instructions for Schedules A&B (Form 1040).

OMB No. 1545-0074

2006

Attachment Sequence No. 07

Name(s) shown on Form 1040

Your social security number

Medical and Dental Expenses		Caution. Do not include expenses reimbursed or paid by others.		
	1	Medical and dental expenses (see page A-1)	1	
	2	Enter amount from Form 1040, line 38 [2]		
	3	Multiply line 2 by 7.5% (.075)	3	
	4	Subtract line 3 from line 1. If line 3 is more than line 1, enter -0-		4
Taxes You Paid (See page A-2.)	5	State and local income taxes	5	
	6	Real estate taxes (see page A-3)	6	
	7	Personal property taxes	7	
	8	Other taxes. List type and amount ▶	8	
	9	Add lines 5 through 8		9
Interest You Paid (See page A-3.)	10	Home mortgage interest and points reported to you on Form 1098	10	
	11	Home mortgage interest not reported to you on Form 1098. If paid to the person from whom you bought the home, see page A-3 and show that person's name, identifying no., and address ▶	11	
Note. Personal interest is not deductible.	12	Points not reported to you on Form 1098. See page A-4 for special rules	12	
	13	Investment interest. Attach Form 4952 if required. (See page A-4.)	13	
	14	Add lines 10 through 13		14
Gifts to Charity	15	Gifts by cash or check. If you made any gift of $250 or more, see page A-5	15	
If you made a gift and got a benefit for it, see page A-4.	16	Other than by cash or check. If any gift of $250 or more, see page A-5. You must attach Form 8283 if over $500	16	
	17	Carryover from prior year	17	
	18	Add lines 15 through 17		18
Casualty and Theft Losses	19	Casualty or theft loss(es). Attach Form 4684. (See page A-6.)		19
Job Expenses and Certain Miscellaneous Deductions (See page A-6.)	20	Unreimbursed employee expenses—job travel, union dues, job education, etc. Attach Form 2106 or 2106-EZ if required. (See page A-6.) ▶	20	
	21	Tax preparation fees	21	
	22	Other expenses—investment, safe deposit box, etc. List type and amount ▶	22	
	23	Add lines 20 through 22	23	
	24	Enter amount from Form 1040, line 38 [24]		
	25	Multiply line 24 by 2% (.02)	25	
	26	Subtract line 25 from line 23. If line 25 is more than line 23, enter -0-		26
Other Miscellaneous Deductions	27	Other—from list on page A-7. List type and amount ▶		27
Total Itemized Deductions	28	Is Form 1040, line 38, over $150,500 (over $75,250 if married filing separately)? ☐ No. Your deduction is not limited. Add the amounts in the far right column for lines 4 through 27. Also, enter this amount on Form 1040, line 40. ▶ ☐ Yes. Your deduction may be limited. See page A-7 for the amount to enter.		28
	29	If you elect to itemize deductions even though they are less than your standard deduction, check here ▶ ☐		

SCHEDULE SE (Form 1040)

Department of the Treasury Internal Revenue Service

Self-Employment Tax

▶ Attach to Form 1040. ▶ See Instructions for Schedule SE (Form 1040).

OMB No. 1545-0074

2006

Attachment Sequence No. 17

Name of person with self-employment income (as shown on Form 1040)

Social security number of person with self-employment income ▶

Who Must File Schedule SE

You must file Schedule SE if:

- You had net earnings from self-employment from other than church employee income (line 4 of Short Schedule SE or line 4c of Long Schedule SE) of $400 or more, or
- You had church employee income of $108.28 or more. Income from services you performed as a minister or a member of a religious order **is not** church employee income (see page SE-1).

Note. Even if you had a loss or a small amount of income from self-employment, it may be to your benefit to file Schedule SE and use either "optional method" in Part II of Long Schedule SE (see page SE-3).

Exception. If your only self-employment income was from earnings as a minister, member of a religious order, or Christian Science practitioner **and** you filed Form 4361 and received IRS approval not to be taxed on those earnings, **do not** file Schedule SE. Instead, write "Exempt–Form 4361" on Form 1040, line 58.

May I Use Short Schedule SE or Must I Use Long Schedule SE?

Note. Use this flowchart **only** if you must file Schedule SE. If unsure, see *Who Must File Schedule SE*, above.

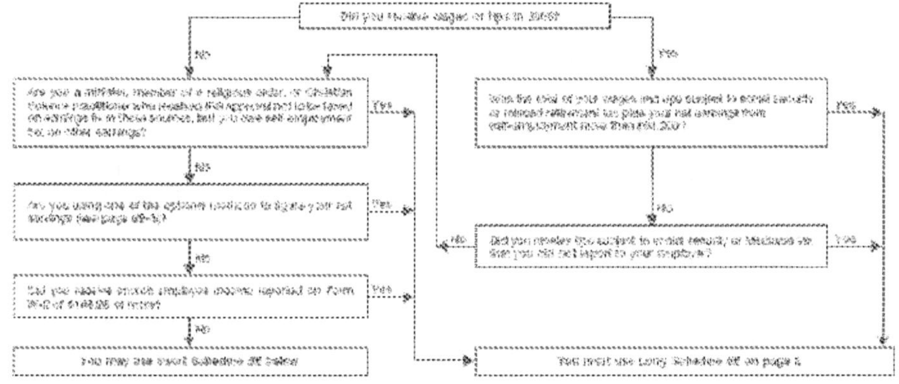

Section A—Short Schedule SE. Caution. *Read above to see if you can use Short Schedule SE.*

1	Net farm profit or (loss) from Schedule F, line 36, and farm partnerships, Schedule K-1 (Form 1065), box 14, code A	1	
2	Net profit or (loss) from Schedule C, line 31; Schedule C-EZ, line 3; Schedule K-1 (Form 1065), box 14, code A (other than farming); and Schedule K-1 (Form 1065-B), box 9, code J1. Ministers and members of religious orders, see page SE-1 for amounts to report on this line. See page SE-3 for other income to report	2	
3	Combine lines 1 and 2	3	
4	Net earnings from self-employment. Multiply line 3 by 92.35% (.9235). If less than $400, do not file this schedule; you do not owe self-employment tax ▶	4	
5	Self-employment tax. If the amount on line 4 is: • $94,200 or less, multiply line 4 by 15.3% (.153). Enter the result here and on Form 1040, line 58. • More than $94,200, multiply line 4 by 2.9% (.029). Then, add $11,680.80 to the result. Enter the total here and on Form 1040, line 58.	5	
6	Deduction for one-half of self-employment tax. Multiply line 5 by 50% (.5). Enter the result here and on Form 1040, line 27 — 6		

For Paperwork Reduction Act Notice, see Form 1040 instructions. Cat. No. 11358Z Schedule SE (Form 1040) 2006

Schedule SE (Form 1040) 2006 — Attachment Sequence No. 17 — Page 2

Name of person with self-employment income (as shown on Form 1040) | Social security number of person with self-employment income ▶

Section B—Long Schedule SE

Part I Self-Employment Tax

Note. If your only income subject to self-employment tax is church employee income, skip lines 1 through 4b. Enter -0- on line 4c and go to line 5a. Income from services you performed as a minister or a member of a religious order is not church employee income. See page SE-1.

A If you are a minister, member of a religious order, or Christian Science practitioner and you filed Form 4361, but you had $400 or more of other net earnings from self-employment, check here and continue with Part I . . . ▶ ☐

1	Net farm profit or (loss) from Schedule F, line 36, and farm partnerships, Schedule K-1 (Form 1065), box 14, code A. **Note.** Skip this line if you use the farm optional method (see page SE-4)	1	
2	Net profit or (loss) from Schedule C, line 31; Schedule C-EZ, line 3; Schedule K-1 (Form 1065), box 14, code A (other than farming); and Schedule K-1 (Form 1065-B), box 9, code J1. Ministers and members of religious orders, see page SE-1 for amounts to report on this line. See page SE-3 for other income to report. **Note.** Skip this line if you use the nonfarm optional method (see page SE-4)	2	
3	Combine lines 1 and 2 . . .	3	
4a	If line 3 is more than zero, multiply line 3 by 92.35% (.9235). Otherwise, enter amount from line 3	4a	
b	If you elect one or both of the optional methods, enter the total of lines 15 and 17 here . . .	4b	
c	Combine lines 4a and 4b. If less than $400, stop; you do not owe self-employment tax. **Exception.** If less than $400 and you had church employee income, enter -0- and continue . . . ▶	4c	
5a	Enter your church employee income from Form W-2. See page SE-1 for definition of church employee income . . .	5a	
b	Multiply line 5a by 92.35% (.9235). If less than $100, enter -0- . . .	5b	
6	Net earnings from self-employment. Add lines 4c and 5b . . .	6	
7	Maximum amount of combined wages and self-employment earnings subject to social security tax or the 6.2% portion of the 7.65% railroad retirement (tier 1) tax for 2006 . . .	7	94,200 00
8a	Total social security wages and tips (total of boxes 3 and 7 on Form(s) W-2) and railroad retirement (tier 1) compensation. If $94,200 or more, skip lines 8b through 10, and go to line 11 . . .	8a	
b	Unreported tips subject to social security tax (from Form 4137, line 9)	8b	
c	Add lines 8a and 8b . . .	8c	
9	Subtract line 8c from line 7. If zero or less, enter -0- here and on line 10 and go to line 11 . ▶	9	
10	Multiply the smaller of line 6 or line 9 by 12.4% (.124) . . .	10	
11	Multiply line 6 by 2.9% (.029) . . .	11	
12	Self-employment tax. Add lines 10 and 11. Enter here and on Form 1040, line 58 . . .	12	
13	Deduction for one-half of self-employment tax. Multiply line 12 by 50% (.5). Enter the result here and on Form 1040, line 27 . . .	13	

Part II Optional Methods To Figure Net Earnings (see page SE-4)

Farm Optional Method. You may use this method only if (a) your gross farm income[1] was not more than $2,400, or (b) your net farm profits[2] were less than $1,733.

14	Maximum income for optional methods . . .	14	1,600 00
15	Enter the smaller of: two-thirds (⅔) of gross farm income[1] (not less than zero) or $1,600. Also include this amount on line 4b above . . .	15	

Nonfarm Optional Method. You may use this method only if (a) your net nonfarm profits[3] were less than $1,733 and also less than 72.189% of your gross nonfarm income[4] and (b) you had net earnings from self-employment of at least $400 in 2 of the prior 3 years.

Caution. You may use this method no more than five times.

16	Subtract line 15 from line 14 . . .	16	
17	Enter the smaller of: two-thirds (⅔) of gross nonfarm income[4] (not less than zero) or the amount on line 16. Also include this amount on line 4b above . . .	17	

[1] From Sch. F, line 11, and Sch. K-1 (Form 1065), box 14, code B.

[2] From Sch. F, line 36, and Sch. K-1 (Form 1065), box 14, code A.

[3] From Sch. C, line 31; Sch. C-EZ, line 3; Sch. K-1 (Form 1065), box 14, code A; and Sch. K-1 (Form 1065-B), box 9, code J1.

[4] From Sch. C, line 7; Sch. C-EZ, line 1; Sch. K-1 (Form 1065), box 14, code C; and Sch. K-1 (Form 1065-B), box 9, code J2.

Form **SS-8**
(Rev. November 2006)
Department of the Treasury
Internal Revenue Service

Determination of Worker Status for Purposes of Federal Employment Taxes and Income Tax Withholding

OMB No. 1545-0004

Name of firm (or person) for whom the worker performed services		Worker's name	
Firm's address (include street address, apt. or suite no., city, state, and ZIP code)		Worker's address (include street address, apt. or suite no., city, state, and ZIP code)	
Trade name		Daytime telephone number ( )	Worker's social security number
Telephone number (include area code) ( )	Firm's employer identification number	Worker's employer identification number (if any)	

Note. If the worker is paid by a firm other than the one listed on this form for these services, enter the name, address, and employer identification number of the payer. ►

Disclosure of Information

The information provided on Form SS-8 may be disclosed to the firm, worker, or payer named above to assist the IRS in the determination process. For example, if you are a worker, we may disclose the information you provide on Form SS-8 to the firm or payer named above. The information can only be disclosed to assist with the determination process. If you provide incomplete information, we may not be able to process your request. See *Privacy Act and Paperwork Reduction Act Notice* on page 5 for more information. If you do not want this information disclosed to other parties, do not file Form SS-8.

Parts I–V. All filers of Form SS-8 must complete all questions in Parts I–IV. Part V must be completed if the worker provides a service directly to customers or is a salesperson. If you cannot answer a question, enter "Unknown" or "Does not apply." If you need more space for a question, attach another sheet with the part and question number clearly identified.

Part I General Information

1 This form is being completed by: ☐ Firm ☐ Worker; for services performed .... to ....
(beginning date) (ending date)

2 Explain your reason(s) for filing this form (for example, you received a bill from the IRS, you believe you erroneously received a Form 1099 or Form W-2, you are unable to get worker's compensation benefits, or you were audited or are being audited by the IRS). ....

3 Total number of workers who performed or are performing the same or similar services ....

4 How did the worker obtain the job? ☐ Application ☐ Bid ☐ Employment Agency ☐ Other (specify) ....

5 Attach copies of all supporting documentation (contracts, invoices, memos, Forms W-2 or Forms 1099-MISC issued or received, IRS closing agreements, IRS rulings, etc.). In addition, please inform us of any current or past litigation concerning the worker's status. If no income reporting forms (Form 1099-MISC or W-2) were furnished to the worker, enter the amount of income earned for the year(s) at issue $........................

If both Form W-2 and Form 1099-MISC were issued or received, explain why. ....

6 Describe the firm's business. ....

7 Describe the work done by the worker and provide the worker's job title. ....

8 Explain why you believe the worker is an employee or an independent contractor. ....

9 Did the worker perform services for the firm in any capacity before providing the services that are the subject of this determination request?
☐ Yes ☐ No ☐ N/A
If "Yes," what were the dates of the prior service? ....
If "Yes," explain the differences, if any, between the current and prior service. ....

10 If the work is done under a written agreement between the firm and the worker, attach a copy (preferably signed by both parties). Describe the terms and conditions of the work arrangement. ....

Part II Behavioral Control

1 What specific training and/or instruction is the worker given by the firm?

2 How does the worker receive work assignments?

3 Who determines the methods by which the assignments are performed?

4 Who is the worker required to contact if problems or complaints arise and who is responsible for their resolution?

5 What types of reports are required from the worker? Attach examples.

6 Describe the worker's daily routine such as, schedule, hours, etc.

7 At what location(s) does the worker perform services (e.g., firm's premises, own shop or office, home, customer's location, etc.)? Indicate the appropriate percentage of time the worker spends in each location, if more than one.

8 Describe any meetings the worker is required to attend and any penalties for not attending (e.g., sales meetings, monthly meetings, staff meetings, etc.).

9 Is the worker required to provide the services personally? ☐ Yes ☐ No

10 If substitutes or helpers are needed, who hires them?

11 If the worker hires the substitutes or helpers, is approval required? ☐ Yes ☐ No
If "Yes," by whom?

12 Who pays the substitutes or helpers?

13 Is the worker reimbursed if the worker pays the substitutes or helpers? ☐ Yes ☐ No
If "Yes," by whom?

Part III Financial Control

1 List the supplies, equipment, materials, and property provided by each party:
The firm
The worker
Other party

2 Does the worker lease equipment? ☐ Yes ☐ No
If "Yes," what are the terms of the lease? (Attach a copy or explanatory statement.)

3 What expenses are incurred by the worker in the performance of services for the firm?

4 Specify which, if any, expenses are reimbursed by:
The firm
Other party

5 Type of pay the worker receives: ☐ Salary ☐ Commission ☐ Hourly Wage ☐ Piece Work
☐ Lump Sum ☐ Other (specify)
If type of pay is commission, and the firm guarantees a minimum amount of pay, specify amount $

6 Is the worker allowed a drawing account for advances? ☐ Yes ☐ No
If "Yes," how often?
Specify any restrictions.

7 Whom does the customer pay? ☐ Firm ☐ Worker
If worker, does the worker pay the total amount to the firm? ☐ Yes ☐ No If "No," explain.

8 Does the firm carry worker's compensation insurance on the worker? ☐ Yes ☐ No

9 What economic loss or financial risk, if any, can the worker incur beyond the normal loss of salary (e.g., loss or damage of equipment, material, etc.)?

Part IV Relationship of the Worker and Firm

1 List the benefits available to the worker (e.g., paid vacations, sick pay, pensions, bonuses, paid holidays, personal days, insurance benefits).

2 Can the relationship be terminated by either party without incurring liability or penalty? ☐ Yes ☐ No

If "No," explain your answer.

3 Did the worker perform similar services for others during the same time period? ☐ Yes ☐ No

If "Yes," is the worker required to get approval from the firm? ☐ Yes ☐ No

4 Describe any agreements prohibiting competition between the worker and the firm while the worker is performing services or during any later period. Attach any available documentation.

5 Is the worker a member of a union? ☐ Yes ☐ No

6 What type of advertising, if any, does the worker do (e.g., a business listing in a directory, business cards, etc.)? Provide copies, if applicable.

7 If the worker assembles or processes a product at home, who provides the materials and instructions or pattern?

8 What does the worker do with the finished product (e.g., return it to the firm, provide it to another party, or sell it)?

9 How does the firm represent the worker to its customers (e.g., employee, partner, representative, or contractor)?

10 If the worker no longer performs services for the firm, how did the relationship end (e.g., worker quit or was fired, job completed, contract ended, firm or worker went out of business)?

Part V For Service Providers or Salespersons. Complete this part if the worker provided a service directly to customers or is a salesperson.

1 What are the worker's responsibilities in soliciting new customers?

2 Who provides the worker with leads to prospective customers?

3 Describe any reporting requirements pertaining to the leads.

4 What terms and conditions of sale, if any, are required by the firm?

5 Are orders submitted to and subject to approval by the firm? ☐ Yes ☐ No

6 Who determines the worker's territory?

7 Did the worker pay for the privilege of serving customers on the route or in the territory? ☐ Yes ☐ No

If "Yes," whom did the worker pay?

If "Yes," how much did the worker pay? $

8 Where does the worker sell the product (e.g., in a home, retail establishment, etc.)?

9 List the product and/or services distributed by the worker (e.g., meat, vegetables, fruit, bakery products, beverages, or laundry or dry cleaning services). If more than one type of product and/or service is distributed, specify the principal one.

10 Does the worker sell life insurance full time? ☐ Yes ☐ No

11 Does the worker sell other types of insurance for the firm? ☐ Yes ☐ No

If "Yes," enter the percentage of the worker's total working time spent in selling other types of insurance %

12 If the worker solicits orders from wholesalers, retailers, contractors, or operators of hotels, restaurants, or other similar establishments, enter the percentage of the worker's time spent in the solicitation %

13 Is the merchandise purchased by the customers for resale or use in their business operations? ☐ Yes ☐ No

Describe the merchandise and state whether it is equipment installed on the customers' premises.

Sign Here Under penalties of perjury, I declare that I have examined this request, including accompanying documents, and to the best of my knowledge and belief, the facts presented are true, correct, and complete.

▶ Type or print name below signature. Title ▶ Date ▶

DO NOT STAPLE

33333

For Official Use Only

Telephone number

Fax number

For Official Use Only

Form **W-3** Transmittal of Wage and Tax Statements **2007**

Send this entire page with the entire Copy A page of Form(s) W-2 to the Social Security Administration. Photocopies are not acceptable.

Do not send any payment (cash, checks, money orders, etc.) with Forms W-2 and W-3.

Form **941 for 2007: Employer's QUARTERLY Federal Tax Return** 950107

(Rev. January 2007) Department of the Treasury — Internal Revenue Service OMB No. 1545-0029

(EIN) Employer identification number [ ][ ] – [ ][ ][ ][ ][ ][ ][ ]

Name *(not your trade name)*

Trade name *(if any)*

Address

Number Street Suite or room number

City State ZIP code

Report for this Quarter of 2007 (Check one.)

- ☐ 1: January, February, March
- ☐ 2: April, May, June
- ☐ 3: July, August, September
- ☐ 4: October, November, December

Read the separate instructions before you fill out this form. Please type or print within the boxes.

Part 1: Answer these questions for this quarter.

1 **Number of employees who received wages, tips, or other compensation for the pay period including:** ***Mar. 12*** **(Quarter 1),** ***June 12*** **(Quarter 2),** ***Sept. 12*** **(Quarter 3),** ***Dec. 12*** **(Quarter 4)** . . . 1

2 **Wages, tips, and other compensation** . . . 2

3 **Total income tax withheld from wages, tips, and other compensation** . . . 3

4 **If no wages, tips, and other compensation are subject to social security or Medicare tax** . . ☐ Check and go to line 6.

5 **Taxable social security and Medicare wages and tips:**

	Column 1		*Column 2*
5a **Taxable social security wages**	.	× .124 =	.
5b **Taxable social security tips**	.	× .124 =	.
5c **Taxable Medicare wages & tips**	.	× .029 =	.

5d **Total social security and Medicare taxes** (*Column 2*, lines 5a + 5b + 5c = line 5d) . . 5d

6 **Total taxes before adjustments** (lines 3 + 5d = line 6) . . . 6

7 **TAX ADJUSTMENTS** (Read the instructions for line 7 before completing lines 7a through 7h.):

7a **Current quarter's fractions of cents** . . .

7b **Current quarter's sick pay** . . .

7c **Current quarter's adjustments for tips and group-term life insurance**

7d **Current year's income tax withholding** (attach Form 941c) . . .

7e **Prior quarters' social security and Medicare taxes** (attach Form 941c)

7f **Special additions to federal income tax** (attach Form 941c) . . .

7g **Special additions to social security and Medicare** (attach Form 941c)

7h **TOTAL ADJUSTMENTS** (Combine all amounts: lines 7a through 7g.) . . . 7h

8 **Total taxes after adjustments** (Combine lines 6 and 7h.) . . . 8

9 **Advance earned income credit (EIC) payments made to employees** . . . 9

10 **Total taxes after adjustment for advance EIC** (line 8 – line 9 = line 10) . . . 10

11 **Total deposits for this quarter, including overpayment applied from a prior quarter** . . . 11

12 **Balance due** (If line 10 is more than line 11, write the difference here.) . . . 12
Follow the Instructions for Form 941-V, Payment Voucher.

13 **Overpayment** (If line 11 is more than line 10, write the difference here.) . Check one ☐ Apply to next return. ☐ Send a refund.

▶ You **MUST** fill out both pages of this form and **SIGN** it.

Next ➔

For Privacy Act and Paperwork Reduction Act Notice, see the back of the Payment Voucher. Cat. No. 17001Z Form **941** (Rev. 1-2007)

950207

Name (not your trade name) | Employer identification number (EIN)

Part 2: Tell us about your deposit schedule and tax liability for this quarter.

If you are unsure about whether you are a monthly schedule depositor or a semiweekly schedule depositor, see *Pub. 15* (Circular E), section 11.

14 ☐☐ Write the state abbreviation for the state where you made your deposits OR write "MU" if you made your deposits in *multiple* states.

15 Check one: ☐ Line 10 is less than $2,500. Go to Part 3.

☐ You were a monthly schedule depositor for the entire quarter. Fill out your tax liability for each month. Then go to Part 3.

Tax liability: Month 1 ______ .

Month 2 ______ .

Month 3 ______ .

Total liability for quarter ______ . Total must equal line 10.

☐ You were a semiweekly schedule depositor for any part of this quarter. Fill out Schedule B (Form 941): *Report of Tax Liability for Semiweekly Schedule Depositors,* and attach it to this form.

Part 3: Tell us about your business. If a question does NOT apply to your business, leave it blank.

16 If your business has closed or you stopped paying wages . . . . ☐ Check here, and

enter the final date you paid wages ___/___/___

17 If you are a seasonal employer and you do not have to file a return for every quarter of the year . . ☐ Check here.

Part 4: May we speak with your third-party designee?

Do you want to allow an employee, a paid tax preparer, or another person to discuss this return with the IRS? (See the instructions for details.)

☐ Yes. Designee's name ______

Select a 5-digit Personal Identification Number (PIN) to use when talking to IRS. ☐☐☐☐☐

☐ No.

Part 5: Sign here. You MUST fill out both pages of this form and SIGN it.

Under penalties of perjury, I declare that I have examined this return, including accompanying schedules and statements, and to the best of my knowledge and belief, it is true, correct, and complete.

Sign your name here ______ Print your name here ______

Print your title here ______

Date ___/___/___ Best daytime phone (___) ___ - ____

Part 6: For paid preparers only (optional)

Paid Preparer's Signature ______

Firm's name ______

Address ______ EIN ______

ZIP code ______

Date ___/___/___ Phone (___) ___ - ____ SSN/PTIN ______

☐ Check if you are self-employed.

Form **1040-ES**
Department of the Treasury
Internal Revenue Service

2007 Payment Voucher **1**

OMB No. 1545-0074

File only if you are making a payment of estimated tax by check or money order. Mail this voucher with your check or money order payable to the "United States Treasury." Write your social security number and "2007 Form 1040-ES" on your check or money order. Do not send cash. Enclose, but do not staple or attach, your payment with this voucher.

Calendar year—Due April 17, 2007

Amount of estimated tax you are paying by check or money order. Dollars | Cents

Print or type

Your first name and initial	Your last name	Your social security number
If joint payment, complete for spouse		
Spouse's first name and initial	Spouse's last name	Spouse's social security number
Address (number, street, and apt. no.)		
City, state, and ZIP code. (If a foreign address, enter city, province or state, postal code, and country.)		

For Privacy Act and Paperwork Reduction Act Notice, see instructions on page 5.

SCHEDULE C (Form 1040)

Department of the Treasury Internal Revenue Service (99)

Profit or Loss From Business

(Sole Proprietorship)

▶ Partnerships, joint ventures, etc., must file Form 1065 or 1065-B.

▶ Attach to Form 1040, 1040NR, or 1041. ▶ See Instructions for Schedule C (Form 1040).

OMB No. 1545-0074

2006

Attachment Sequence No. 09

Name of proprietor | Social security number (SSN)

A Principal business or profession, including product or service (see page C-2 of the instructions) | B Enter code from pages C-8, 9, & 10 ▶

C Business name. If no separate business name, leave blank. | D Employer ID number (EIN), if any

E Business address (including suite or room no.) ▶
City, town or post office, state, and ZIP code

F Accounting method: (1) ☐ Cash (2) ☐ Accrual (3) ☐ Other (specify) ▶

G Did you "materially participate" in the operation of this business during 2006? If "No," see page C-3 for limit on losses ☐ Yes ☐ No

H If you started or acquired this business during 2006, check here ▶ ☐

Part I Income

1	Gross receipts or sales. Caution. If this income was reported to you on Form W-2 and the "Statutory employee" box on that form was checked, see page C-3 and check here ▶ ☐	1	
2	Returns and allowances	2	
3	Subtract line 2 from line 1	3	
4	Cost of goods sold (from line 42 on page 2)	4	
5	Gross profit. Subtract line 4 from line 3	5	
6	Other income, including federal and state gasoline or fuel tax credit or refund (see page C-3)	6	
7	Gross income. Add lines 5 and 6 ▶	7	

Part II Expenses. Enter expenses for business use of your home only on line 30.

8	Advertising	8		18	Office expense	18	
9	Car and truck expenses (see page C-4)	9		19	Pension and profit-sharing plans	19	
10	Commissions and fees	10		20	Rent or lease (see page C-5):		
11	Contract labor (see page C-4)	11			a Vehicles, machinery, and equipment	20a	
12	Depletion	12			b Other business property	20b	
13	Depreciation and section 179 expense deduction (not included in Part III) (see page C-4)	13		21	Repairs and maintenance	21	
				22	Supplies (not included in Part III)	22	
				23	Taxes and licenses	23	
				24	Travel, meals, and entertainment:		
					a Travel	24a	
14	Employee benefit programs (other than on line 19)	14			b Deductible meals and entertainment (see page C-5)	24b	
15	Insurance (other than health)	15		25	Utilities	25	
16	Interest:			26	Wages (less employment credits)	26	
	a Mortgage (paid to banks, etc.)	16a		27	Other expenses (from line 48 on page 2)	27	
	b Other	16b					
17	Legal and professional services	17					

28	Total expenses before expenses for business use of home. Add lines 8 through 27 in columns ▶	28	
29	Tentative profit (loss). Subtract line 28 from line 7	29	
30	Expenses for business use of your home. Attach Form 8829	30	
31	Net profit or (loss). Subtract line 30 from line 29. • If a profit, enter on both Form 1040, line 12, and Schedule SE, line 2, or on Form 1040NR, line 13 (statutory employees, see page C-6). Estates and trusts, enter on Form 1041, line 3. • If a loss, you must go to line 32.	31	
32	If you have a loss, check the box that describes your investment in this activity (see page C-6). • If you checked 32a, enter the loss on both Form 1040, line 12, and Schedule SE, line 2, or on Form 1040NR, line 13 (statutory employees, see page C-6). Estates and trusts, enter on Form 1041, line 3. • If you checked 32b, you must attach Form 6198. Your loss may be limited.		32a ☐ All investment is at risk. 32b ☐ Some investment is not at risk.

For Paperwork Reduction Act Notice, see page C-8 of the instructions. Cat. No. 11334P Schedule C (Form 1040) 2006

9595 ☐ VOID ☐ CORRECTED

PAYER'S name, street address, city, state, ZIP code, and telephone no.		1 Rents $	OMB No. 1545-0115 **2007** Form 1099-MISC	**Miscellaneous Income**
		2 Royalties $		
		3 Other income $	4 Federal income tax withheld $	**Copy A** For Internal Revenue Service Center File with Form 1096.
PAYER'S federal identification number	RECIPIENT'S identification number	5 Fishing boat proceeds $	6 Medical and health care payments $	
RECIPIENT'S name		7 Nonemployee compensation $	8 Substitute payments in lieu of dividends or interest $	For Privacy Act and Paperwork Reduction Act Notice, see the 2007 General Instructions for Forms 1099, 1098, 5498, and W-2G.
Street address (including apt. no.)		9 Payer made direct sales of $5,000 or more of consumer products to a buyer (recipient) for resale ► ☐	10 Crop insurance proceeds $	
City, state, and ZIP code		11	12	
Account number (see instructions)	2nd TIN not. ☐	13 Excess golden parachute payments $	14 Gross proceeds paid to an attorney $	
15a Section 409A deferrals $	15b Section 409A income $	16 State tax withheld $ $	17 State/Payer's state no.	18 State income $ $

Form **1099-MISC** Cat. No. 14425J Department of the Treasury - Internal Revenue Service

Do Not Cut or Separate Forms on This Page — Do Not Cut or Separate Forms on This Page

22222	Void ☐	a Employee's social security number	For Official Use Only ▶ OMB No. 1545-0008

b Employer identification number (EIN)	1 Wages, tips, other compensation	2 Federal income tax withheld
c Employer's name, address, and ZIP code	3 Social security wages	4 Social security tax withheld
	5 Medicare wages and tips	6 Medicare tax withheld
	7 Social security tips	8 Allocated tips
d Control number	9 Advance EIC payment	10 Dependent care benefits
e Employee's first name and initial / Last name / Suff.	11 Nonqualified plans	12a See instructions for box 12
	13 Statutory employee ☐ Retirement plan ☐ Third-party sick pay ☐	12b
	14 Other	12c
f Employee's address and ZIP code		12d

15 State	Employer's state ID number	16 State wages, tips, etc.	17 State income tax	18 Local wages, tips, etc.	19 Local income tax	20 Locality name

Form **W-2** Wage and Tax Statement **2007**

Department of the Treasury—Internal Revenue Service

For Privacy Act and Paperwork Reduction Act Notice, see back of Copy D.

Copy A For Social Security Administration — Send this entire page with Form W-3 to the Social Security Administration; photocopies are not acceptable.

Cat. No. 10134D

Do Not Cut, Fold, or Staple Forms on This Page — Do Not Cut, Fold, or Staple Forms on This Page

Form W-4 (2007)

Purpose. Complete Form W-4 so that your employer can withhold the correct federal income tax from your pay. Because your tax situation may change, you may want to refigure your withholding each year.

Exemption from withholding. If you are exempt, complete only lines 1, 2, 3, 4, and 7 and sign the form to validate it. Your exemption for 2007 expires February 16, 2008. See Pub. 505, Tax Withholding and Estimated Tax.

Note. You cannot claim exemption from withholding if (a) your income exceeds $850 and includes more than $300 of unearned income (for example, interest and dividends) and (b) another person can claim you as a dependent on their tax return.

Basic instructions. If you are not exempt, complete the Personal Allowances Worksheet below. The worksheets on page 2 adjust your withholding allowances based on itemized deductions, certain credits, adjustments to income, or two-earner/multiple job situations. Complete all worksheets that apply. However, you may claim fewer (or zero) allowances.

Head of household. Generally, you may claim head of household filing status on your tax return only if you are unmarried and pay more than 50% of the costs of keeping up a home for yourself and your dependent(s) or other qualifying individuals.

Tax credits. You can take projected tax credits into account in figuring your allowable number of withholding allowances. Credits for child or dependent care expenses and the child tax credit may be claimed using the Personal Allowances Worksheet below. See Pub. 919, How Do I Adjust My Tax Withholding, for information on converting your other credits into withholding allowances.

Nonwage income. If you have a large amount of nonwage income, such as interest or dividends, consider making estimated tax payments using Form 1040-ES, Estimated Tax for Individuals. Otherwise, you may owe additional tax. If you have pension or annuity income, see Pub. 919 to find out if you should adjust your withholding on Form W-4 or W-4P.

Two earners/Multiple jobs. If you have a working spouse or more than one job, figure the total number of allowances you are entitled to claim on all jobs using worksheets from only one Form W-4. Your withholding usually will be most accurate when all allowances are claimed on the Form W-4 for the highest paying job and zero allowances are claimed on the others.

Nonresident alien. If you are a nonresident alien, see the Instructions for Form 8233 before completing this Form W-4.

Check your withholding. After your Form W-4 takes effect, use Pub. 919 to see how the dollar amount you are having withheld compares to your projected total tax for 2007. See Pub. 919, especially if your earnings exceed $130,000 (Single) or $180,000 (Married).

Personal Allowances Worksheet (Keep for your records.)

A Enter "1" for yourself if no one else can claim you as a dependent . . . . A ______

B Enter "1" if:
- You are single and have only one job; or
- You are married, have only one job, and your spouse does not work; or
- Your wages from a second job or your spouse's wages (or the total of both) are $1,000 or less.

. . . B ______

C Enter "1" for your spouse. But, you may choose to enter "-0-" if you are married and have either a working spouse or more than one job. (Entering "-0-" may help you avoid having too little tax withheld.) . . . . C ______

D Enter number of dependents (other than your spouse or yourself) you will claim on your tax return . . . . . . D ______

E Enter "1" if you will file as head of household on your tax return (see conditions under Head of household above) . E ______

F Enter "1" if you have at least $1,500 of child or dependent care expenses for which you plan to claim a credit . . F ______

(Note. Do not include child support payments. See Pub. 503, Child and Dependent Care Expenses, for details.)

G Child Tax Credit (including additional child tax credit). See Pub. 972, Child Tax Credit, for more information.
- If your total income will be less than $57,000 ($85,000 if married), enter "2" for each eligible child.
- If your total income will be between $57,000 and $84,000 ($85,000 and $119,000 if married), enter "1" for each eligible child plus "1" additional if you have 4 or more eligible children. G ______

H Add lines A through G and enter total here. (Note. This may be different from the number of exemptions you claim on your tax return.) ► H ______

For accuracy, complete all worksheets that apply.
- If you plan to itemize or claim adjustments to income and want to reduce your withholding, see the Deductions and Adjustments Worksheet on page 2.
- If you have more than one job or are married and you and your spouse both work and the combined earnings from all jobs exceed $40,000 ($25,000 if married) see the Two-Earners/Multiple Jobs Worksheet on page 2 to avoid having too little tax withheld.
- If neither of the above situations applies, stop here and enter the number from line H on line 5 of Form W-4 below.

Cut here and give Form W-4 to your employer. Keep the top part for your records.

Form **W-4** | **Employee's Withholding Allowance Certificate** | OMB No. 1545-0074 **2007**

Department of the Treasury Internal Revenue Service

► Whether you are entitled to claim a certain number of allowances or exemption from withholding is subject to review by the IRS. Your employer may be required to send a copy of this form to the IRS.

1 Type or print your first name and middle initial. | Last name | 2 Your social security number

Home address (number and street or rural route) | 3 ☐ Single ☐ Married ☐ Married, but withhold at higher Single rate.
Note. If married, but legally separated, or spouse is a nonresident alien, check the "Single" box.

City or town, state, and ZIP code | 4 If your last name differs from that shown on your social security card, check here. You must call 1-800-772-1213 for a replacement card. ► ☐

5 Total number of allowances you are claiming (from line H above or from the applicable worksheet on page 2) | 5 |

6 Additional amount, if any, you want withheld from each paycheck . . . . | 6 | $

7 I claim exemption from withholding for 2007, and I certify that I meet both of the following conditions for exemption.
- Last year I had a right to a refund of all federal income tax withheld because I had no tax liability and
- This year I expect a refund of all federal income tax withheld because I expect to have no tax liability.

If you meet both conditions, write "Exempt" here . . . . ► | 7 |

Under penalties of perjury, I declare that I have examined this certificate and to the best of my knowledge and belief, it is true, correct, and complete.

Employee's signature
(Form is not valid
unless you sign it.) ► Date ►

8 Employer's name and address (Employer: Complete lines 8 and 10 only if sending to the IRS.) | 9 Office code (optional) | 10 Employer identification number (EIN)

For Privacy Act and Paperwork Reduction Act Notice, see page 2. Cat. No. 10220Q Form **W-4** (2007)

Form **2106** | **Employee Business Expenses** | OMB No. 1545-0074

Department of the Treasury
Internal Revenue Service [illegible]

▶ See separate instructions.

▶ Attach to Form 1040 or Form 1040NR.

2006
Attachment Sequence No. 54

Your name | Occupation in which you incurred expenses | Social security number

Part I Employee Business Expenses and Reimbursements

Step 1 Enter Your Expenses		Column A Other Than Meals and Entertainment	Column B Meals and Entertainment
1 Vehicle expense from line 22 or line 29. (Rural mail carriers: See instructions.)	1		
2 Parking fees, tolls, and transportation, including train, bus, etc., that did not involve overnight travel or commuting to and from work	2		
3 Travel expense while away from home overnight, including lodging, airplane, car rental, etc. Do not include meals and entertainment	3		
4 Business expenses not included on lines 1 through 3. Do not include meals and entertainment	4		
5 Meals and entertainment expenses (see instructions)	5		
6 Total expenses. In Column A, add lines 1 through 4 and enter the result. In Column B, enter the amount from line 5	6		

Note: If you were not reimbursed for any expenses in Step 1, skip line 7 and enter the amount from line 6 on line 8.

Step 2 Enter Reimbursements Received From Your Employer for Expenses Listed in Step 1			
7 Enter reimbursements received from your employer that were not reported to you in box 1 of Form W-2. Include any reimbursements reported under code "L" in box 12 of your Form W-2 (see instructions)	7		

Step 3 Figure Expenses To Deduct on Schedule A (Form 1040)			
8 Subtract line 7 from line 6. If zero or less, enter -0-. However, if line 7 is greater than line 6 in Column A, report the excess as income on Form 1040, line 7 (or on Form 1040NR, line 8)	8		
Note: If both columns of line 8 are zero, you cannot deduct employee business expenses. Stop here and attach Form 2106 to your return.			
9 In Column A, enter the amount from line 8. In Column B, multiply line 8 by 50% (.50). (Employees subject to Department of Transportation (DOT) hours of service limits: Multiply meal expenses incurred while away from home on business by 75% (.75) instead of 50%. For details, see instructions.)	9		
10 Add the amounts on line 9 of both columns and enter the total here. Also, enter the total on Schedule A (Form 1040), line 20 (or on Schedule A (Form 1040NR), line 9). (Reservists, qualified performing artists, fee-basis state or local government officials, and individuals with disabilities: See the instructions for special rules on where to enter the total.) ▶	10		

For Paperwork Reduction Act Notice, see instructions. Cat. No. [illegible] Form 2106 [illegible]

Form 2106 (2006) Page 2

Part II Vehicle Expenses

Section A—General Information (You must complete this section if you are claiming vehicle expenses.)		(a) Vehicle 1	(b) Vehicle 2
11 Enter the date the vehicle was placed in service	11	/ /	/ /
12 Total miles the vehicle was driven during 2006	12	miles	miles
13 Business miles included on line 12	13	miles	miles
14 Percent of business use. Divide line 13 by line 12	14	%	%
15 Average daily roundtrip commuting distance	15	miles	miles
16 Commuting miles included on line 12	16	miles	miles
17 Other miles. Add lines 13 and 16 and subtract the total from line 12	17	miles	miles

18 Do you (or your spouse) have another vehicle available for personal use? ☐ Yes ☐ No

19 Was your vehicle available for personal use during off-duty hours? ☐ Yes ☐ No

20 Do you have evidence to support your deduction? ☐ Yes ☐ No

21 If "Yes," is the evidence written? ☐ Yes ☐ No

Section B—Standard Mileage Rate (See the instructions for Part II to find out whether to complete this section or Section C.)

22 Multiply line 13 by 44.5¢ (.445)	22	

Section C—Actual Expenses		(a) Vehicle 1	(b) Vehicle 2
23 Gasoline, oil, repairs, vehicle insurance, etc.	23		
24a Vehicle rentals	24a		
b Inclusion amount (see instructions)	24b		
c Subtract line 24b from line 24a	24c		
25 Value of employer-provided vehicle (applies only if 100% of annual lease value was included on Form W-2—see instructions)	25		
26 Add lines 23, 24c, and 25	26		
27 Multiply line 26 by the percentage on line 14	27		
28 Depreciation (see instructions)	28		
29 Add lines 27 and 28. Enter total here and on line 1	29		

Section D—Depreciation of Vehicles (Use this section only if you owned the vehicle and are completing Section C for the vehicle.)		(a) Vehicle 1	(b) Vehicle 2
30 Enter cost or other basis (see instructions)	30		
31 Enter section 179 deduction (see instructions)	31		
32 Multiply line 30 by line 14 (see instructions if you claimed the section 179 deduction or special allowance)	32		
33 Enter depreciation method and percentage (see instructions)	33		
34 Multiply line 32 by the percentage on line 33 (see instructions)	34		
35 Add lines 31 and 34	35		
36 Enter the applicable limit explained in the line 36 instructions	36		
37 Multiply line 36 by the percentage on line 14	37		
38 Enter the smaller of line 35 or line 37. If you skipped lines 36 and 37, enter the amount from line 35. Also enter this amount on line 28 above	38		

Form 2106 (2006)

Form **4361**
(Rev. November 2005)
Department of the Treasury
Internal Revenue Service

Application for Exemption From Self-Employment Tax for Use by Ministers, Members of Religious Orders and Christian Science Practitioners

OMB No. 1545-0074

File Original and Two Copies

File original and two copies and attach supporting documents. This exemption is granted only if the IRS returns a copy to you marked "approved."

Please type or print	1 Name of taxpayer applying for exemption (as shown on Form 1040)	Social security number
	Number and street (including apt. no.)	Telephone number (optional) ( )
	City or town, state, and ZIP code	

2 Check one box: ☐ Christian Science practitioner ☐ Ordained minister, priest, rabbi ☐ Member of religious order not under a vow of poverty ☐ Commissioned or licensed minister (see line 6)

3 Date ordained, licensed, etc. (Attach supporting document. See instructions.) / /

4 Legal name of ordaining, licensing, or commissioning body or religious order

Number, street, and room or suite no. — Employer identification number

City or town, state, and ZIP code

5 Enter the first 2 years, after the date shown on line 3, that you had net self-employment earnings of $400 or more, any of which came from services as a minister, priest, rabbi, etc.; member of a religious order; or Christian Science practitioner ▶

6 If you apply for the exemption as a licensed or commissioned minister, and your denomination also ordains ministers, please indicate how your ecclesiastical powers differ from those of an ordained minister of your denomination. Attach a copy of your denomination's bylaws relating to the powers of ordained, commissioned, and licensed ministers.

7 I certify that I am conscientiously opposed to, or because of my religious principles I am opposed to, the acceptance (for services I perform as a minister, member of a religious order not under a vow of poverty, or a Christian Science practitioner) of any public insurance that makes payments in the event of death, disability, old age, or retirement; or that makes payments toward the cost of, or provides services for, medical care. (Public insurance includes insurance systems established by the Social Security Act.)

I certify that as a duly ordained, commissioned, or licensed minister of a church or a member of a religious order not under a vow of poverty, I have informed the ordaining, commissioning, or licensing body of my church or order that I am conscientiously opposed to, or because of religious principles I am opposed to the acceptance (for services I perform as a minister or as a member of a religious order) of any public insurance that makes payments in the event of death, disability, old age, or retirement; or that makes payments toward the cost of, or provides services for, medical care, including the benefits of any insurance system established by the Social Security Act.

I certify that I have never filed Form 2031 to revoke a previous exemption from social security coverage on earnings as a minister, member of a religious order not under a vow of poverty, or a Christian Science practitioner.

I request to be exempted from paying self-employment tax on my earnings from services as a minister, member of a religious order not under a vow of poverty, or a Christian Science practitioner, under section 1402(e) of the Internal Revenue Code. I understand that the exemption, if granted, will apply only to these earnings. Under penalties of perjury, I declare that I have examined this application and to the best of my knowledge and belief, it is true and correct.

Signature ▶ Date ▶

Caution: Form 4361 is not proof of the right to an exemption from Federal income tax withholding or social security tax, the right to a parsonage allowance exclusion (section 107 of the Internal Revenue Code), assignment by your religious superiors to a particular job, or the exemption or church status of the ordaining, licensing, or commissioning body, or religious order.

For Internal Revenue Service Use

☐ Approved for exemption from self-employment tax on ministerial earnings
☐ Disapproved for exemption from self-employment tax on ministerial earnings

By .... (Director's signature) .... (Date)

General Instructions

Section references are to the Internal Revenue Code.

Purpose of form. File Form 4361 to apply for an exemption from self-employment tax if you are:

- An ordained, commissioned, or licensed minister of a church;
- A member of a religious order who has not taken a vow of poverty;
- A Christian Science practitioner; or
- A commissioned or licensed minister of a church or church denomination that ordains ministers, if you have authority to perform substantially all religious duties of your church or denomination.

This application must be based on your religious or conscientious opposition to the acceptance (for services performed as a minister, member of a religious order not under a vow of poverty, or Christian Science practitioner) of any public insurance that makes payments for death, disability, old age, or retirement; or that makes payments for the cost of, or provides services for, medical care, including any insurance benefits established by the Social Security Act.

If you are a duly ordained, commissioned, or licensed minister of a church or a member of a religious order not under a vow of poverty, prior to filing this form you must inform the ordaining, commissioning, or licensing body of your church or order that you are opposed to the acceptance of public insurance benefits based on ministerial service on religious or conscientious grounds.

Form **4029**
(Rev. April 2008)
Department of the Treasury
Internal Revenue Service

Application for Exemption From Social Security and Medicare Taxes and Waiver of Benefits

▶ Before you file this form, see the instructions under Who may apply on page 2.
▶ Do not use prior versions of this form.

OMB No. 1545-0064

File Three Copies

Caution: Approval of Form 4029 exempts you from social security and Medicare taxes only. The exemption does not apply to federal income tax. Ministers, members of religious orders, and Christian Science practitioners, see Form 4361, Application for Exemption From Self-Employment Tax for Use by Ministers, Members of Religious Orders, and Christian Science Practitioners.

Part I To Be Completed by Applicant (Print or type)

Print or type

1 Name of taxpayer	2 Social security number
Address (number, street, or P.O. box)	3 Date of birth
City or town, state, and ZIP code	4 Contact phone number ( )

5 ☐ Do not send me my social security statement.

I certify that I am and continuously have been a member of .... (Name of religious group)

.... (Religious district or congregation, and county and/or city, state, and ZIP code)

since .... (Month) (Day) (Year), and as a follower of the established teachings of that group, I am conscientiously opposed to accepting benefits of any private or public insurance that makes payments in the event of death, disability, old age, or retirement; or makes payments for the cost of medical care; or provides services for medical care. Public insurance includes any insurance system established by the Social Security Act.

I request that I be exempted from paying social security and Medicare taxes on my earnings from self-employment under Internal Revenue Code section 1402 and from the employer's share of social security and Medicare taxes under Internal Revenue Code section 3111.

I further request exemption from the employee's share of social security and Medicare taxes under Internal Revenue Code section 3101, for my services as an employee whenever I am employed by an employer who has an identical exemption from social security and Medicare taxes.

I waive all rights to any social security payment or benefit under Titles II and XVIII of the Social Security Act. I understand and agree that no benefits or other payments of any kind under Titles II and XVIII of the Social Security Act will be paid based on my wages and self-employment income to any other person. I certify that I have never received benefits or payments under the above titles, nor has anyone else received these benefits based on my earnings.

I agree to notify the Internal Revenue Service within 60 days of any occurrence that results in my no longer being a member of the religious group described above, or no longer following the established teachings of this group. See Where to file on page 2.

Furthermore, I understand that if the tax exemption for myself or for my employer under sections 1402(g) or 3127 of the Internal Revenue Code is no longer effective, this waiver will also no longer be effective for:

- Myself, with respect to all my wages and self-employment income; and
- My employees, with respect to wages I may pay to them; and that if my employer's exemption is no longer in effect, my exemption will end with respect to wages paid to me by my employer. However, the waiver will no longer be effective only to the extent that benefits and other payments under Titles II and XVIII of the Social Security Act can be payable on the basis of:
- My self-employment income for and after the first tax year in which the exemption ends; and
- My wages for and after the calendar year following the calendar year in which the employer no longer meets the requirements of section 1402(g) or 3127 on which the end of the exemption is based.

Under penalties of perjury, I declare that I have examined this application and waiver, and to the best of my knowledge and belief, it is true and correct.

Signature of Applicant ▶ .... Date ▶ ....

Part II To Be Completed by Authorized Representative of Religious Group (Print or type)

I certify that .... (Name of taxpayer) is a member of .... (Name of religious group/district/congregation)

Name of Authorized Representative .... (Please print or type) .... (Address)

Signature of Authorized Representative ▶ .... Title ▶ .... Date ▶ ....

Social Security Administration Use Only

☐ This religious group is recognized as being in existence continuously since December 31, 1950, as providing a reasonable level of living for its dependent members, and as being conscientiously opposed to public or private insurance.

☐ This religious group is not recognized as being in existence continuously since December 31, 1950, as providing a reasonable level of living for its dependent members, and/or as being conscientiously opposed to public or private insurance.

Signature of Authorized SSA Representative ▶ .... Date ▶ ....

Internal Revenue Service Use Only

☐ Approved for exemption from social security and Medicare taxes. (See Caution in Part I above.)
☐ Disapproved for exemption from social security and Medicare taxes.

Signature and Title of Authorized IRS Representative ▶ .... Date ▶ ....

For Privacy Act and Paperwork Reduction Act Notice, see page 2. Cat. No. 41277 Form **4029** (Rev. 4-2008)

Sample Income Tax Return

a Control number	22222	Void ☐	For Official Use Only ▶ OMB No. 1545-0008

b Employer identification number (EIN)	00-0244010
c Employer's name, address, and ZIP code	First United Church 1040 Main Street Hometown, Texas 77090
d Employee's social security number	00-00-2222
e Employee's first name and initial	John E.
Last name	Minister
f Employee's address and ZIP code	1040 Main Street Hometown, TX 77090
1 Wages, tips, other compensation	31000.00
2 Federal income tax withheld	[illegible]
3 Social security wages	
4 Social security tax withheld	
5 Medicare wages and tips	
6 Medicare tax withheld	
7 Social security tips	
8 Allocated tips	
9 Advance EIC payment	
10 Dependent care benefits	
11 Nonqualified plans	
12a See instructions for box 12	
12b	
12c	
12d	
13 Statutory employee / Retirement plan / Third-party sick pay	☐ ☐ ☐
14 Other	Parsonage Allowance 9600.00 Utilities Allowance 1200.00
15 State / Employer's state ID number	
16 State wages, tips, etc.	
17 State income tax	
18 Local wages, tips, etc.	
19 Local income tax	
20 Locality name	

Form **W-2** Wage and Tax Statement **2006**

Department of the Treasury—Internal Revenue Service

For Privacy Act and Paperwork Reduction Act Notice, see back of Copy D.

Copy A For Social Security Administration — Send this entire page with Form W-3 to the Social Security Administration; photocopies are not acceptable.

Cat. No. 10134D

a Control number	22222	Void ☐	For Official Use Only ▶ OMB No. 1545-0008

b Employer identification number (EIN)	00-0337225
c Employer's name, address, and ZIP code	Hometown College 40 Hope Road Hometown, Texas 77090
d Employee's social security number	00-00-2222
e Employee's first name and initial	John E.
Last name	Minister
f Employee's address and ZIP code	1040 Main Street Hometown, TX 77090
1 Wages, tips, other compensation	3400.00
2 Federal income tax withheld	272.00
3 Social security wages	3400.00
4 Social security tax withheld	210.80
5 Medicare wages and tips	3400.00
6 Medicare tax withheld	49.30
7 Social security tips	
8 Allocated tips	
9 Advance EIC payment	
10 Dependent care benefits	
11 Nonqualified plans	
12a See instructions for box 12	
12b	
12c	
12d	
13 Statutory employee / Retirement plan / Third-party sick pay	☐ ☐ ☐
14 Other	
15 State / Employer's state ID number	
16 State wages, tips, etc.	
17 State income tax	
18 Local wages, tips, etc.	
19 Local income tax	
20 Locality name	

Form **W-2** Wage and Tax Statement **2006**

Department of the Treasury—Internal Revenue Service

For Privacy Act and Paperwork Reduction Act Notice, see back of Copy D.

Copy A For Social Security Administration — Send this entire page with Form W-3 to the Social Security Administration; photocopies are not acceptable.

Cat. No. 10134D

Form 1040 — Department of the Treasury—Internal Revenue Service — U.S. Individual Income Tax Return 2006

(99) IRS Use Only—Do not write or staple in this space.

For the year Jan. 1–Dec. 31, 2006, or other tax year beginning , 2006, ending , 20 — OMB No. 1545-0074

Label (See instructions on page 16.) Use the IRS label. Otherwise, please print or type.

Your first name and initial: John E.	Last name: Michaels	Your social security number: 011 : 00 : 2222
If a joint return, spouse's first name and initial: Susan R.	Last name: Michaels	Spouse's social security number: 011 : 00 : 1111
Home address (number and street). If you have a P.O. box, see page 16.: 1040 Main Street	Apt. no.	▲ You must enter your SSN(s) above. ▲
City, town or post office, state, and ZIP code. If you have a foreign address, see page 16.: Hometown, TX 77099		Checking a box below will not change your tax or refund.

Presidential Election Campaign ▶ Check here if you, or your spouse if filing jointly, want $3 to go to this fund (see page 16) ▶ [X] You [X] Spouse

Filing Status

Check only one box.

1 [ ] Single
2 [X] Married filing jointly (even if only one had income)
3 [ ] Married filing separately. Enter spouse's SSN above and full name here. ▶
4 [ ] Head of household (with qualifying person). (See page 17.) If the qualifying person is a child but not your dependent, enter this child's name here. ▶
5 [ ] Qualifying widow(er) with dependent child (see page 17)

Exemptions

6a [X] Yourself. If someone can claim you as a dependent, do not check box 6a — Boxes checked on 6a and 6b: 2
b [X] Spouse

c Dependents:

(1) First name Last name	(2) Dependent's social security number	(3) Dependent's relationship to you	(4) ✓ if qualifying child for child tax credit (see page 19)
Jennifer Michaels	111 : 00 : 1113	daughter	[X]
			[ ]
			[ ]
			[ ]

If more than four dependents, see page 19.

No. of children on 6c who: • lived with you: 1
• did not live with you due to divorce or separation (see page 20):
Dependents on 6c not entered above:

d Total number of exemptions claimed — Add numbers on lines above ▶ 3

Income

Attach Form(s) W-2 here. Also attach Forms W-2G and 1099-R if tax was withheld.

If you did not get a W-2, see page 23.

Enclose, but do not attach, any payment. Also, please use Form 1040-V.

7	Wages, salaries, tips, etc. Attach Form(s) W-2 — Excess Allowance $240	7	34,640
8a	Taxable interest. Attach Schedule B if required	8a	
b	Tax-exempt interest. Do not include on line 8a	8b	
9a	Ordinary dividends. Attach Schedule B if required	9a	
b	Qualified dividends (see page 23)	9b	
10	Taxable refunds, credits, or offsets of state and local income taxes (see page 24)	10	
11	Alimony received	11	
12	Business income or (loss). Attach Schedule C or C-EZ	12	3,781
13	Capital gain or (loss). Attach Schedule D if required. If not required, check here ▶ [ ]	13	
14	Other gains or (losses). Attach Form 4797	14	
15a	IRA distributions 15a — b Taxable amount (see page 25)	15b	
16a	Pensions and annuities 16a — b Taxable amount (see page 26)	16b	
17	Rental real estate, royalties, partnerships, S corporations, trusts, etc. Attach Schedule E	17	
18	Farm income or (loss). Attach Schedule F	18	
19	Unemployment compensation	19	
20a	Social security benefits 20a — b Taxable amount (see page 27)	20b	
21	Other income. List type and amount (see page 29)	21	
22	Add the amounts in the far right column for lines 7 through 21. This is your total income ▶	22	38,421

Adjusted Gross Income

23	Archer MSA deduction. Attach Form 8853	23			
24	Certain business expenses of reservists, performing artists, and fee-basis government officials. Attach Form 2106 or 2106-EZ	24			
25	Health savings account deduction. Attach Form 8889	25			
26	Moving expenses. Attach Form 3903	26			
27	One-half of self-employment tax. Attach Schedule SE	27	3,120		
28	Self-employed SEP, SIMPLE, and qualified plans	28			
29	Self-employed health insurance deduction (see page 29)	29			
30	Penalty on early withdrawal of savings	30			
31a	Alimony paid b Recipient's SSN ▶	31a			
32	IRA deduction (see page 31)	32			
33	Student loan interest deduction (see page 33)	33			
34	Jury duty pay you gave to your employer	34			
35	Domestic production activities deduction. Attach Form 8903	35			
36	Add lines 23 through 31a and 32 through 35			36	3,120
37	Subtract line 36 from line 22. This is your adjusted gross income ▶			37	35,301

For Disclosure, Privacy Act, and Paperwork Reduction Act Notice, see page 80. Cat. No. 11320B Form 1040 (2006)

Form 1040 (2006) Page 2

Tax and Credits

38	Amount from line 37 (adjusted gross income)	38	35,505
39a	Check if: ☐ You were born before January 2, 1942, ☐ Blind. ☐ Spouse was born before January 2, 1942, ☐ Blind. Total boxes checked ▶ 39a		
b	If your spouse itemizes on a separate return or you were a dual-status alien, see page 34 and check here ▶39b ☐		
40	Itemized deductions (from Schedule A) or your standard deduction (see left margin)	40	12,???
41	Subtract line 40 from line 38	41	21,505
42	If line 38 is over $112,875, or you provided housing to a person displaced by Hurricane Katrina, see page 36. Otherwise, multiply $3,300 by the total number of exemptions claimed on line 6d	42	9,900
43	Taxable income. Subtract line 42 from line 41. If line 42 is more than line 41, enter -0-	43	11,705
44	Tax (see page 36). Check if any tax is from: a ☐ Form(s) 8814 b ☐ Form 4972	44	1,175
45	Alternative minimum tax (see page 39). Attach Form 6251	45	
46	Add lines 44 and 45 ▶	46	1,175
47	Foreign tax credit. Attach Form 1116 if required	47	
48	Credit for child and dependent care expenses. Attach Form 2441	48	
49	Credit for the elderly or the disabled. Attach Schedule R	49	
50	Education credits. Attach Form 8863	50	
51	Retirement savings contributions credit. Attach Form 8880	51	
52	Residential energy credits. Attach Form 5695	52	
53	Child tax credit (see page 42). Attach Form 8901 if required	53	1,000
54	Credits from: a ☐ Form 8396 b ☐ Form 8839 c ☐ Form 8859	54	
55	Other credits: a ☐ Form 3800 b ☐ Form 8801 c ☐ Form ____	55	
56	Add lines 47 through 55. These are your total credits	56	1,000
57	Subtract line 56 from line 46. If line 56 is more than line 46, enter -0- ▶	57	175

Standard Deduction for— • People who checked any box on line 39a or 39b or who can be claimed as a dependent, see page 34. • All others: Single or Married filing separately, $5,150; Married filing jointly or Qualifying widow(er), $10,300; Head of household, $7,550

Other Taxes

58	Self-employment tax. Attach Schedule SE	58	6,240
59	Social security and Medicare tax on tip income not reported to employer. Attach Form 4137	59	
60	Additional tax on IRAs, other qualified retirement plans, etc. Attach Form 5329 if required	60	
61	Advance earned income credit payments from Form(s) W-2, box 9	61	
62	Household employment taxes. Attach Schedule H	62	
63	Add lines 57 through 62. This is your total tax ▶	63	6,415

Payments

64	Federal income tax withheld from Forms W-2 and 1099	64	272
65	2006 estimated tax payments and amount applied from 2005 return	65	8,400
66a	Earned income credit (EIC)	66a	
b	Nontaxable combat pay election ▶ 66b		
67	Excess social security and tier 1 RRTA tax withheld (see page 60)	67	
68	Additional child tax credit. Attach Form 8812	68	
69	Amount paid with request for extension to file (see page 60)	69	
70	Payments from: a ☐ Form 2439 b ☐ Form 4136 c ☐ Form 8885	70	
71	Credit for federal telephone excise tax paid. Attach Form 8913 if required	71	
72	Add lines 64, 65, 66a, and 67 through 71. These are your total payments ▶	72	8,672

If you have a qualifying child, attach Schedule EIC.

Refund

73	If line 72 is more than line 63, subtract line 63 from line 72. This is the amount you overpaid	73	2,257
74a	Amount of line 73 you want refunded to you. If Form 8888 is attached, check here ▶	74a	
▶ b	Routing number ▶ c Type: ☐ Checking ☐ Savings		
▶ d	Account number		
75	Amount of line 73 you want applied to your 2007 estimated tax ▶	75	2,259

Direct deposit? See page 61 and fill in 74b, 74c, and 74d, or Form 8888.

Amount You Owe

76	Amount you owe. Subtract line 72 from line 63. For details on how to pay, see page 62 ▶	76	
77	Estimated tax penalty (see page 62)	77	

Third Party Designee

Do you want to allow another person to discuss this return with the IRS (see page 63)? ☐ Yes. Complete the following. ☐ No

Designee's name ▶ Phone no. ▶ ( ) Personal identification number (PIN) ▶

Sign Here

Joint return? See page 17. Keep a copy for your records.

Under penalties of perjury, I declare that I have examined this return and accompanying schedules and statements, and to the best of my knowledge and belief, they are true, correct, and complete. Declaration of preparer (other than taxpayer) is based on all information of which preparer has any knowledge.

Your signature	Date	Your occupation	Daytime phone number
John E. Michaels	3/1/2007	Minister	( )
Spouse's signature. If a joint return, both must sign.	**Date**	**Spouse's occupation**	
Susan R. Michaels	3/1/2007	Homemaker	

Paid Preparer's Use Only

Preparer's signature ▶ Date Check if self-employed ☐ Preparer's SSN or PTIN

Firm's name (or yours if self-employed), address, and ZIP code ▶ EIN Phone no. ( )

Form 1040 (2006)

SCHEDULES A&B (Form 1040)
Department of the Treasury Internal Revenue Service (99)

Schedule A—Itemized Deductions

(Schedule B is on back)

▶ Attach to Form 1040. ▶ See Instructions for Schedules A&B (Form 1040).

OMB No. 1545-0074 | **2006** | Attachment Sequence No. 07

Name(s) shown on Form 1040: John E. Michaels and Susan R. Michaels | Your social security number: 011 : 00 : 2222

Medical and Dental Expenses		**Caution.** Do not include expenses reimbursed or paid by others.				
	1	Medical and dental expenses (see page A-1)	1			
	2	Enter amount from Form 1040, line 38 [2]				
	3	Multiply line 2 by 7.5% (.075)	3			
	4	Subtract line 3 from line 1. If line 3 is more than line 1, enter -0-			4	
Taxes You Paid (See page A-3.)	5	State and local income taxes	5			
	6	Real estate taxes (see page A-3)	6	1,750		
	7	Personal property taxes	7			
	8	Other taxes. List type and amount ▶	8			
	9	Add lines 5 through 8			9	1,750
Interest You Paid (See page A-3.)	10	Home mortgage interest and points reported to you on Form 1098	10	6,810		
	11	Home mortgage interest not reported to you on Form 1098. If paid to the person from whom you bought the home, see page A-3 and show that person's name, identifying no., and address ▶	11			
Note. Personal interest is not deductible.	12	Points not reported to you on Form 1098. See page A-4 for special rules	12			
	13	Investment interest. Attach Form 4952 if required. (See page A-4.)	13			
	14	Add lines 10 through 13			14	6,810
Gifts to Charity	15	Gifts by cash or check. If you made any gift of $250 or more, see page A-5	15	4,800		
If you made a gift and got a benefit for it, see page A-4.	16	Other than by cash or check. If any gift of $250 or more, see page A-5. You must attach Form 8283 if over $500	16			
	17	Carryover from prior year	17			
	18	Add lines 15 through 17			18	4,800
Casualty and Theft Losses	19	Casualty or theft loss(es). Attach Form 4684. (See page A-6.)			19	
Job Expenses and Certain Miscellaneous Deductions (See page A-6.)	20	Unreimbursed employee expenses—job travel, union dues, job education, etc. Attach Form 2106 or 2106-EZ if required. (See page A-6.) ▶	20	1,042		
	21	Tax preparation fees	21			
	22	Other expenses—investment, safe deposit box, etc. List type and amount ▶	22			
	23	Add lines 20 through 22	23	1,042		
	24	Enter amount from Form 1040, line 38 [24] 35,301				
	25	Multiply line 24 by 2% (.02)	25	706		
	26	Subtract line 25 from line 23. If line 25 is more than line 23, enter -0-			26	336
Other Miscellaneous Deductions	27	Other—from list on page A-7. List type and amount ▶			27	
Total Itemized Deductions	28	Is Form 1040, line 38, over $150,500 (over $75,250 if married filing separately)? ☒ **No.** Your deduction is not limited. Add the amounts in the far right column for lines 4 through 27. Also, enter this amount on Form 1040, line 40. ☐ **Yes.** Your deduction may be limited. See page A-7 for the amount to enter. ▶			28	13,696
	29	If you elect to itemize deductions even though they are less than your standard deduction, check here ▶ ☐				

For Paperwork Reduction Act Notice, see Form 1040 instructions. Cat. No. 11330X **Schedule A (Form 1040) 2006**

SCHEDULE C-EZ (Form 1040)

Department of the Treasury Internal Revenue Service

Net Profit From Business

(Sole Proprietorship)

▶ Partnerships, joint ventures, etc., must file Form 1065 or 1065-B.
▶ Attach to Form 1040, 1040NR, or 1041. ▶ See Instructions on back.

OMB No. 1545-0074

2006

Attachment Sequence No. 09A

Name of proprietor: John E. Nichols

Social security number (SSN): [illegible]

Part I General Information

You May Use Schedule C-EZ Instead of Schedule C Only If You:

- Had business expenses of $5,000 or less.
- Use the cash method of accounting.
- Did not have an inventory at any time during the year.
- Did not have a net loss from your business.
- Had only one business as either a sole proprietor or statutory employee.

And You:

- Had no employees during the year.
- Are not required to file Form 4562, Depreciation and Amortization, for this business. See the instructions for Schedule C, line 13, on page C-4 to find out if you must file.
- Do not deduct expenses for business use of your home.
- Do not have prior year unallowed passive activity losses from this business.

A Principal business or profession, including product or service: Minister

B Enter code from pages C-8, 9, & 10 ▶ [illegible]

C Business name. If no separate business name, leave blank.

D Employer ID number (EIN), if any

E Business address (including suite or room no.). Address not required if same as on page 1 of your tax return.
1042 Main Street
City, town or post office, state, and ZIP code
Hometown, TX 77099

Part II Figure Your Net Profit

1 Gross receipts. Caution. If this income was reported to you on Form W-2 and the "Statutory employee" box on that form was checked, see Statutory Employees in the instructions for Schedule C, line 1, on page C-3 and check here ▶ ☐ ... 1 4,000

2 Total expenses (see instructions). If more than $5,000, you must use Schedule C ... 2 219*

3 Net profit. Subtract line 2 from line 1. If less than zero, you must use Schedule C. Enter on both Form 1040, line 12, and Schedule SE, line 2, or on Form 1040NR, line 13. (Statutory employees do not report this amount on Schedule SE, line 2. Estates and trusts, enter on Form 1041, line 3.) ... 3 3,781

Part III Information on Your Vehicle. Complete this part only if you are claiming car or truck expenses on line 2.

4 When did you place your vehicle in service for business purposes? (month, day, year) ▶ 7 / 8 / 2005

5 Of the total number of miles you drove your vehicle during 2006, enter the number of miles you used your vehicle for:

a Business 446 b Commuting (see instructions) 0 c Other 7,547

6 Do you (or your spouse) have another vehicle available for personal use? ☒ Yes ☐ No

7 Was your vehicle available for personal use during off-duty hours? ☒ Yes ☐ No

8a Do you have evidence to support your deduction? ☒ Yes ☐ No

b If "Yes," is the evidence written? ☒ Yes ☐ No

For Paperwork Reduction Act Notice, see page 2. Cat. No. 14374D Schedule C-EZ (Form 1040) 2006

*See attached statement

SCHEDULE SE
(Form 1040)
Department of the Treasury Internal Revenue Service (99)

Self-Employment Tax

► Attach to Form 1040. ► See Instructions for Schedule SE (Form 1040).

OMB No. 1545-0074
2006
Attachment Sequence No. 17

Name of person with self-employment income (as shown on Form 1040)	Social security number of person with self-employment income ►	
John E. Michaels		011 ⋮ 00 ⋮ 2222

Who Must File Schedule SE

You must file Schedule SE if:

- You had net earnings from self-employment from other than church employee income (line 4 of Short Schedule SE or line 4c of Long Schedule SE) of $400 or more, or
- You had church employee income of $108.28 or more. Income from services you performed as a minister or a member of a religious order is not church employee income (see page SE-1).

Note. Even if you had a loss or a small amount of income from self-employment, it may be to your benefit to file Schedule SE and use either "optional method" in Part II of Long Schedule SE (see page SE-3).

Exception. If your only self-employment income was from earnings as a minister, member of a religious order, or Christian Science practitioner and you filed Form 4361 and received IRS approval not to be taxed on those earnings, do **not** file Schedule SE. Instead, write "Exempt–Form 4361" on Form 1040, line 58.

May I Use Short Schedule SE or Must I Use Long Schedule SE?

Note. Use this flowchart only if you must file Schedule SE. If unsure, see Who Must File Schedule SE, above.

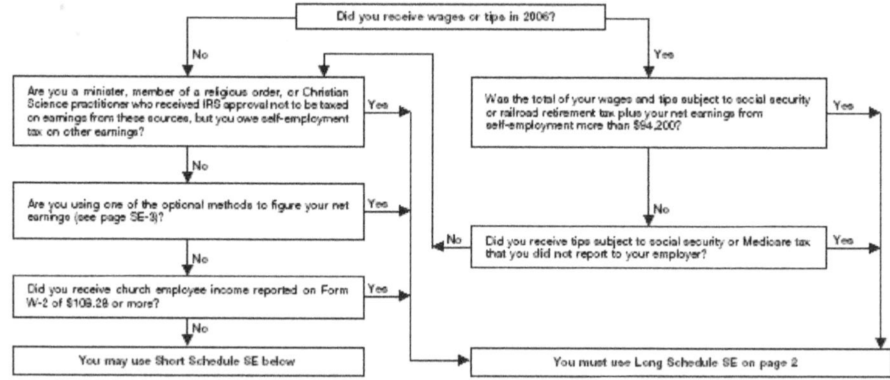

Section A—Short Schedule SE. Caution. Read above to see if you can use Short Schedule SE.

1	Net farm profit or (loss) from Schedule F, line 36, and farm partnerships, Schedule K-1 (Form 1065), box 14, code A	1	
2	Net profit or (loss) from Schedule C, line 31; Schedule C-EZ, line 3; Schedule K-1 (Form 1065), box 14, code A (other than farming); and Schedule K-1 (Form 1065-B), box 9, code J1. Ministers and members of religious orders, see page SE-1 for amounts to report on this line. See page SE-3 for other income to report	2	44,162*
3	Combine lines 1 and 2	3	44,162
4	**Net earnings from self-employment.** Multiply line 3 by 92.35% (.9235). If less than $400, do not file this schedule; you do not owe self-employment tax ►	4	40,784
5	**Self-employment tax.** If the amount on line 4 is: • $94,200 or less, multiply line 4 by 15.3% (.153). Enter the result here and on **Form 1040, line 58.** • More than $94,200, multiply line 4 by 2.9% (.029). Then, add $11,680.80 to the result. Enter the total here and on **Form 1040, line 58.**	5	6,240
6	**Deduction for one-half of self-employment tax.** Multiply line 5 by 50% (.5). Enter the result here and on **Form 1040, line 27** — 6 — 3,120		

*See attached statement.

Form **2106-EZ** | **Unreimbursed Employee Business Expenses** | OMB No. 1545-0074 | **2006**

Department of the Treasury
Internal Revenue Service (99)

▶ Attach to Form 1040 or Form 1040NR.

Attachment Sequence No. 54A

Your name	Occupation in which you incurred expenses	Social security number
John E. Michaels	Minister	[illegible] | 00 | [illegible]

You May Use This Form Only if All of the Following Apply.

- You are an employee deducting ordinary and necessary expenses attributable to your job. An ordinary expense is one that is common and accepted in your field of trade, business, or profession. A necessary expense is one that is helpful and appropriate for your business. An expense does not have to be required to be considered necessary.
- You do not get reimbursed by your employer for any expenses (amounts your employer included in box 1 of your Form W-2 are not considered reimbursements for this purpose).
- If you are claiming vehicle expense, you are using the standard mileage rate for 2006.

Caution: You can use the standard mileage rate for 2006 only if: (a) you owned the vehicle and used the standard mileage rate for the first year you placed the vehicle in service, or (b) you leased the vehicle and used the standard mileage rate for the portion of the lease period after 1997.

Part I Figure Your Expenses

1	Vehicle expense using the standard mileage rate. Complete Part II and multiply line 8a by 44.5¢ (.445)	1	1122
2	Parking fees, tolls, and transportation, including train, bus, etc., that did not involve overnight travel or commuting to and from work	2	
3	Travel expense while away from home overnight, including lodging, airplane, car rental, etc. Do not include meals and entertainment	3	
4	Business expenses not included on lines 1 through 3. Do not include meals and entertainment	4	[illegible]
5	Meals and entertainment expenses: $_______ × 50% (.50) (Employees subject to Department of Transportation (DOT) hours of service limits: Multiply meal expenses incurred while away from home on business by 75% (.75) instead of 50%. For details, see instructions.)	5	
6	Total expenses. Add lines 1 through 5. Enter here and on Schedule A (Form 1040), line 20 (or on Schedule A (Form 1040NR), line 9). (Armed Forces reservists, fee-basis state or local government officials, qualified performing artists, and individuals with disabilities: See the instructions for special rules on where to enter this amount.)	6	[illegible]*

Part II Information on Your Vehicle. Complete this part only if you are claiming vehicle expense on line 1.

7 When did you place your vehicle in service for business use? (month, day, year) ▶ 7 / [illegible] / [illegible]

8 Of the total number of miles you drove your vehicle during 2006, enter the number of miles you used your vehicle for:

a Business 2,521 b Commuting (see instructions) -0- c Other [illegible]

9 Do you (or your spouse) have another vehicle available for personal use? ☒ Yes ☐ No

10 Was your vehicle available for personal use during off-duty hours? ☒ Yes ☐ No

11a Do you have evidence to support your deduction? ☒ Yes ☐ No

b If "Yes," is the evidence written? ☒ Yes ☐ No

For Paperwork Reduction Act Notice, see page 4. Cat. No. 20604Q Form **2106-EZ** (2006)

*See attached statement.

Attachment 1—John E. Michaels 011-00-2222

Worksheet 1. Figuring the Percentage of Tax-Free Income

Note. For each line, enter the appropriate amount in all boxes that are not shaded.

	Source of Income			(a) Taxable	(b) Tax-free	(c) Total
1	W-2 salary as a minister (from box 1 of Form W-2)	1		31,000		31,000
2	Gross income from weddings, baptisms, writing, lecturing, etc. (from line 1 of Schedule C or C-EZ)	2		4,000		4,000
Note. Complete either lines 3a–3e or lines 4a–4i. • If your church provides you with a parsonage, complete lines 3a–3e. • If, instead of providing a parsonage, your church provides you with a rental or parsonage allowance, complete lines 4a–4i.						
3a	FRV* of parsonage provided by church	3a				
b	Utility allowance, if any	3b				
c	Actual expenses for utilities	3c				
d	Enter the smaller of line 3b or 3c	3d				
e	Excess utility allowance (subtract line 3d from line 3b)	3e				
4a	Parsonage or rental allowance	4a	9,600			
b	Utility allowance, if separate	4b	1,200			
c	Total allowance (add lines 4a and 4b)	4c	10,800			
d	Actual expenses for parsonage	4d	9,600			
e	Actual expenses for utilities	4e	960			
f	Total actual expenses for parsonage and utilities (add lines 4d and 4e)	4f	10,560			
g	FRV* of home, plus the cost of utilities	4g	10,800			
h	Enter the smaller of line 4c, 4f, or 4g	4h			10,560	10,560
i	Excess allowance (Subtract line 4h from line 4c)	4i		240		240
5	Ministerial income (for columns (a), (b), and (c), add lines 1 through 4i)	5		35,240	10,560	45,800
6	Percentage of tax-free income:	Total tax-free income $ 10,560 / Total income $ 45,800			=	23 %**

* FRV (Fair Rental Value): as determined objectively and between unrelated parties, what it would cost to rent a comparable home (including furnishings) in a similar location.

** This percentage of your ministerial expenses will not be deductible. Use Worksheets 2 and 3 to figure your allowable deductions.

Attachment 1—John E. Michaels 011-00-2222 *(continued)*

Worksheet 2. **Figuring the Allowable Deduction for Schedule C or C-EZ Expenses**

1	Percentage of expenses that are nondeductible (from Worksheet 1, line 6): 23 %			
2	Business use of car: 445 miles × 44.5¢ (.445)	2		198
3	Meals and entertainment: $______ × 50% (.50)	3		
4	Other expenses (list item and amount)			
a	*Marriage and family booklets*	4a	87	
b		4b		
c		4c		
d		4d		
e		4e		
f	Total other expenses (add lines 4a through 4e)	4f		87
5	Total Schedule C or C-EZ expenses (add lines 2, 3, and 4f)	5		285
6	Nondeductible part of Schedule C or C-EZ expenses (multiply line 5 by the percent in line 1)	6		66
7	Deduction allowed.* Subtract line 6 from line 5. Enter the result here and on Schedule C, line 27, or Schedule C-EZ, line 2.	7		219

* None of the other deductions claimed in this return are allocable to tax-free income.

Worksheet 3. **Figuring the Allowable Deduction for Form 2106 or 2106-EZ Expenses**

1	Percentage of expenses that are nondeductible (from Worksheet 1, line 6): 23 %			
2	Use of car for church business 2,522 miles × 44.5¢ (.445)	2		1,122
3	Meals and entertainment $______ × 50% (.50)	3		
4	Other expenses (list item and amount)			
a	*Professional publications and booklets*	4a	231	
b		4b		
c		4c		
d		4d		
e		4e		
f	Total other expenses (add lines 4a through 4e)	4f		231
5	Total Form 2106 or 2106-EZ expenses (add lines 2, 3, and 4f)	5		1,353
6	Reimbursement not included in box 1 of Form W-2	6		
7	Total unreimbursed Form 2106 or 2106-EZ expenses (subtract line 6 from line 5)	7		1,353
8	Nondeductible part of Form 2106 or 2106-EZ expenses (multiply line 7 by the percent in line 1)	8		311
9	Ministerial employee business expense deduction allowed.* Subtract line 8 from line 7. Enter the result here and on Form 2106, line 10, or Form 2106-EZ, line 6.	9		1,042

* None of the other deductions claimed in this return are allocable to tax-free income.

Attachment 2—John E. Michaels (011-00-2222)

Worksheet 4. Figuring Net Self-Employment Income for Schedule SE (Form 1040)

1	W-2 salary as a minister (from box 1 of Form W-2)	1		31,000
2	Net profit from Schedule C, line 31, or Schedule C-EZ, line 3	2		3,787
3a	Parsonage allowance (from Worksheet 1, line 3a or 4a)	3a	9,600	
b	Utility allowance (from Worksheet 1, line 3b or 4b)	3b	1,200	
c	Total allowance (add lines 3a and 3b)	3c		10,800
4	Add lines 1, 2, and 3c	4		45,587
5	Schedule C or C-EZ expenses allocable to tax-free income (from Worksheet 2, line 8)	5	66	
6	Unreimbursed ministerial employee business expenses (from Worksheet 3, line 7)	6	1,353	
7	Total business expenses not deducted in lines 1 and 2 above (add lines 5 and 6)	7		1,419
8	Net self-employment income. Subtract line 7 from line 4. Enter here and on Schedule SE, Section A, line 2, or Section B, line 2.	8		44,168

Worksheets

These worksheets are provided to help you figure your taxable ministerial income, your allowable deductions, and your net self-employment income.

Worksheet 1. Figuring the Percentage of Tax-Free Income

Note. For each line, enter the appropriate amount in all boxes that are not shaded.

	Source of income			(a) Taxable	(b) Tax-free	(c) Total
1	W-2 salary as a minister (from box 1 of Form W-2)	1				
2	Gross income from weddings, baptisms, writing, lecturing, etc. (from line 1 of Schedule C or C-EZ)	2				
	Note. Complete either lines 3a – 3e or lines 4a – 4i. • If your church provides you with a parsonage, complete lines 3a – 3e. • If, instead of providing a parsonage, your church provides you with a rental or parsonage allowance, complete lines 4a – 4i.					
3a	FRV* of parsonage provided by church	3a				
b	Utility allowance, if any	3b				
c	Actual expenses for utilities	3c				
d	Enter the smaller of line 3b or 3c	3d				
e	Excess utility allowance (subtract line 3d from line 3b)	3e				
4a	Parsonage or rental allowance	4a				
b	Utility allowance, if separate	4b				
c	Total allowance (add lines 4a and 4b)	4c				
d	Actual expenses for parsonage	4d				
e	Actual expenses for utilities	4e				
f	Total actual expenses for parsonage and utilities (add lines 4d and 4e)	4f				
g	FRV* of home, plus the cost of utilities	4g				
h	Enter the smaller of line 4c, 4f, or 4g	4h				
i	Excess allowance (subtract line 4h from line 4c)	4i				
5	Ministerial income (for columns (a), (b), and (c), add lines 1 through 4i)	5				
6	Percentage of tax-free income:	Total tax-free income $ ____ / Total income $ ____		=		%**

* FRV (Fair Rental Value): As determined objectively and between unrelated parties, what it would cost to rent a comparable home (including furnishings) in a similar location.

** This percentage of your ministerial expenses will not be deductible. Use Worksheets 2 and 3 to figure your allowable deductions.

Worksheet 2. **Figuring the Allowable Deduction for Schedule C or C-EZ Expenses**

1	**Percentage of expenses that are nondeductible** (from Worksheet 1, line 6): ________%			
2	Business use of car: ________ miles × 44.5¢ (.445)	2		
3	Meals and entertainment: $________ × 50% (.50)	3		
4	Other expenses (list item and amount)			
a		4a		
b		4b		
c		4c		
d		4d		
e		4e		
f	Total other expenses (add lines 4a through 4e)	4f		
5	Total Schedule C or C-EZ expenses (add lines 2, 3, and 4f)	5		
6	Nondeductible part of Schedule C or C-EZ expenses (multiply line 5 by the percent in line 1)	6		
7	**Deduction allowed.*** Subtract line 6 from line 5. Enter the result here and on Schedule C, line 27, or Schedule C-EZ, line 2.	7		

* None of the other deductions claimed in this return are allocable to tax-free income.

Worksheet 3. **Figuring the Allowable Deduction for Form 2106 or 2106-EZ Expenses**

1	**Percentage of expenses that are nondeductible** (from Worksheet 1, line 6): ________%			
2	Use of car for church business: ________ miles × 44.5¢ (.445)	2		
3	Meals and entertainment: $________ × 50% (.50)	3		
4	Other expenses (list item and amount)			
a		4a		
b		4b		
c		4c		
d		4d		
e		4e		
f	Total other expenses (add lines 4a through 4e)	4f		
5	Total Form 2106 or 2106-EZ expenses (add lines 2, 3, and 4f)	5		
6	Reimbursement not included in box 1 of Form W-2	6		
7	Total unreimbursed Form 2106 or 2106-EZ expenses (subtract line 6 from line 5)	7		
8	Nondeductible part of Form 2106 or 2106-EZ expenses (multiply line 7 by the percent in line 1)	8		
9	**Ministerial employee business expense deduction allowed.*** Subtract line 8 from line 7. Enter the result here and on Form 2106, line 10, or Form 2106-EZ, line 6.	9		

* None of the other deductions claimed in this return are allocable to tax-free income.

Worksheet 4. Figuring Net Self-Employment Income for Schedule SE (Form 1040)

1	W-2 salary as a minister (from box 1 of Form W-2)	1		
2	Net profit from Schedule C, line 31, or Schedule C-EZ, line 3	2		
3a	Parsonage allowance (from Worksheet 1, line 3a or 4a)	3a		
b	Utility allowance (from Worksheet 1, line 3b or 4b)	3b		
c	Total allowance (add lines 3a and 3b)	3c		
4	Add lines 1, 2, and 3c	4		
5	Schedule C or C-EZ expenses allocable to tax-free income (from Worksheet 2, line 6)	5		
6	Unreimbursed ministerial employee business expenses (from Worksheet 3, line 7)	6		
7	Total business expenses not deducted in lines 1 and 2 above (add lines 5 and 6)	7		
8	Net self-employment income. Subtract line 7 from line 4. Enter here and on Schedule SE, Section A, line 2, or Section B, line 5.	8		

www.ingramcontent.com/pod-product-compliance
Lightning Source LLC
Chambersburg PA
CBHW080546170426
43195CB00016B/2701
* 9 7 8 0 9 7 9 6 4 8 2 2 9 *